VINTAGE POSTCARDS STYLE COLORING BOOKS

HALLOWEEN CATS

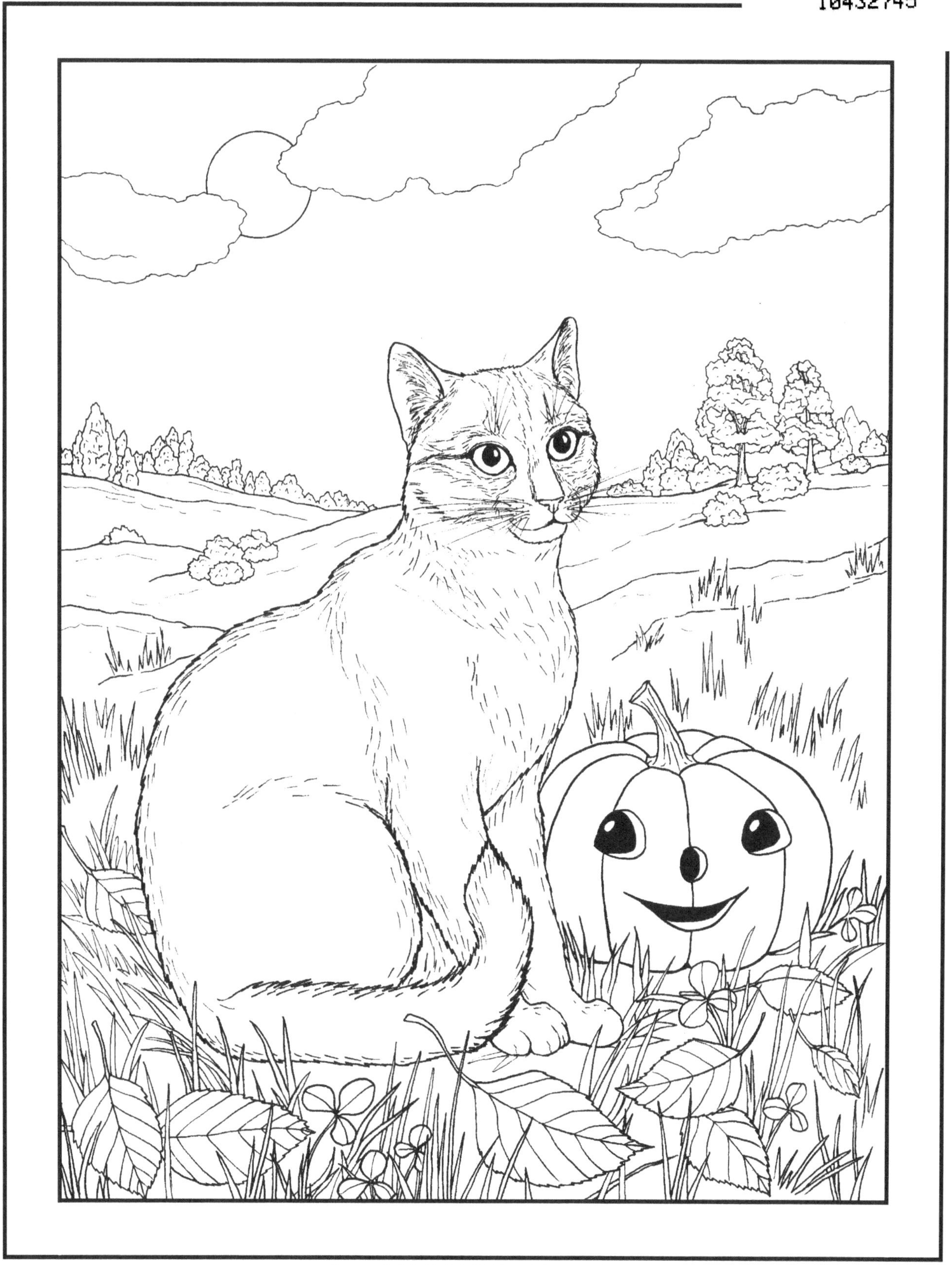

Copyright © 2017 by Alexandra
All rights reserved. No part of this book may be reproduced or transmitted in any form or by electronic or mechanical means, including information storage and retrieval systems, without permission in writing from the author.

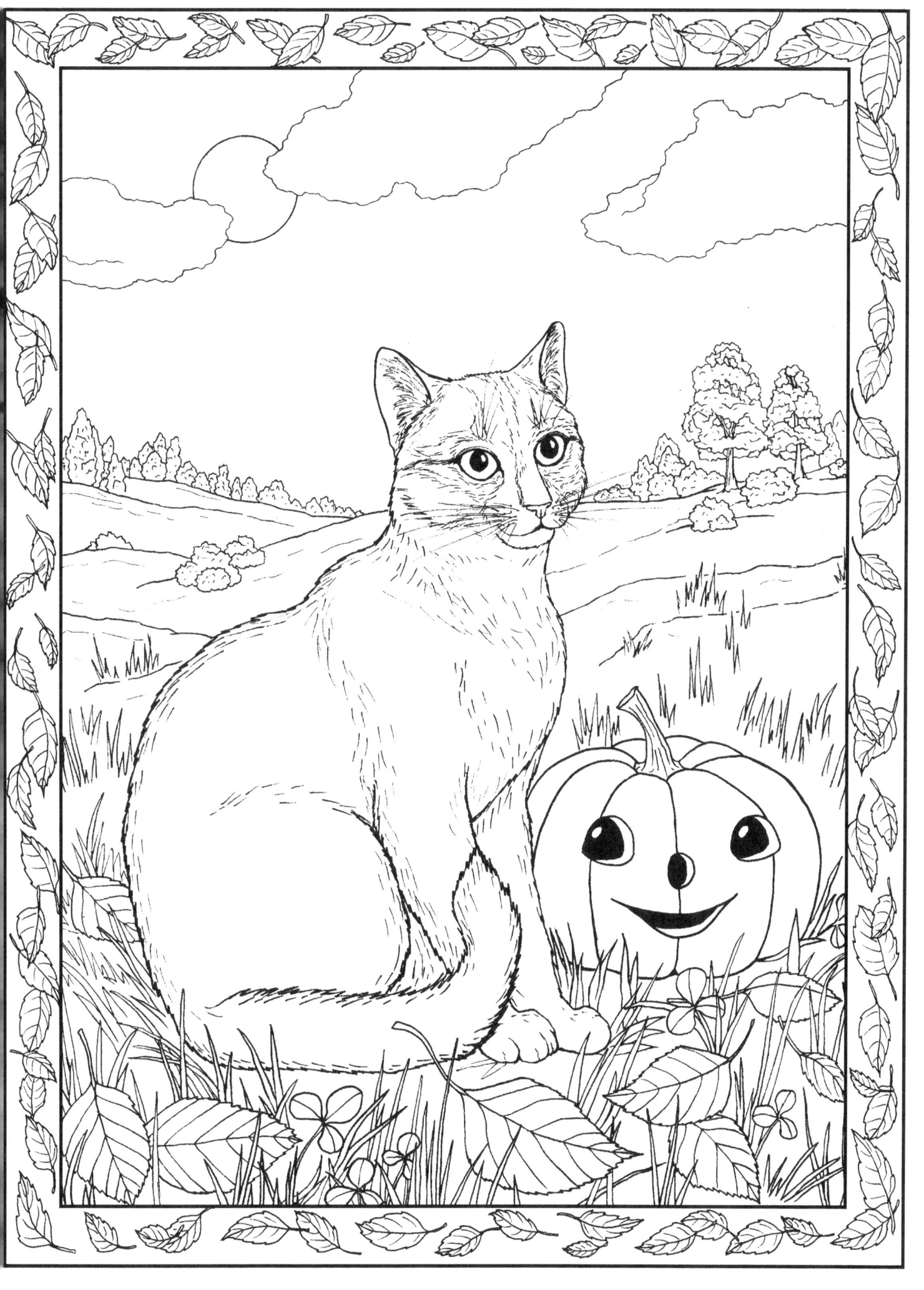

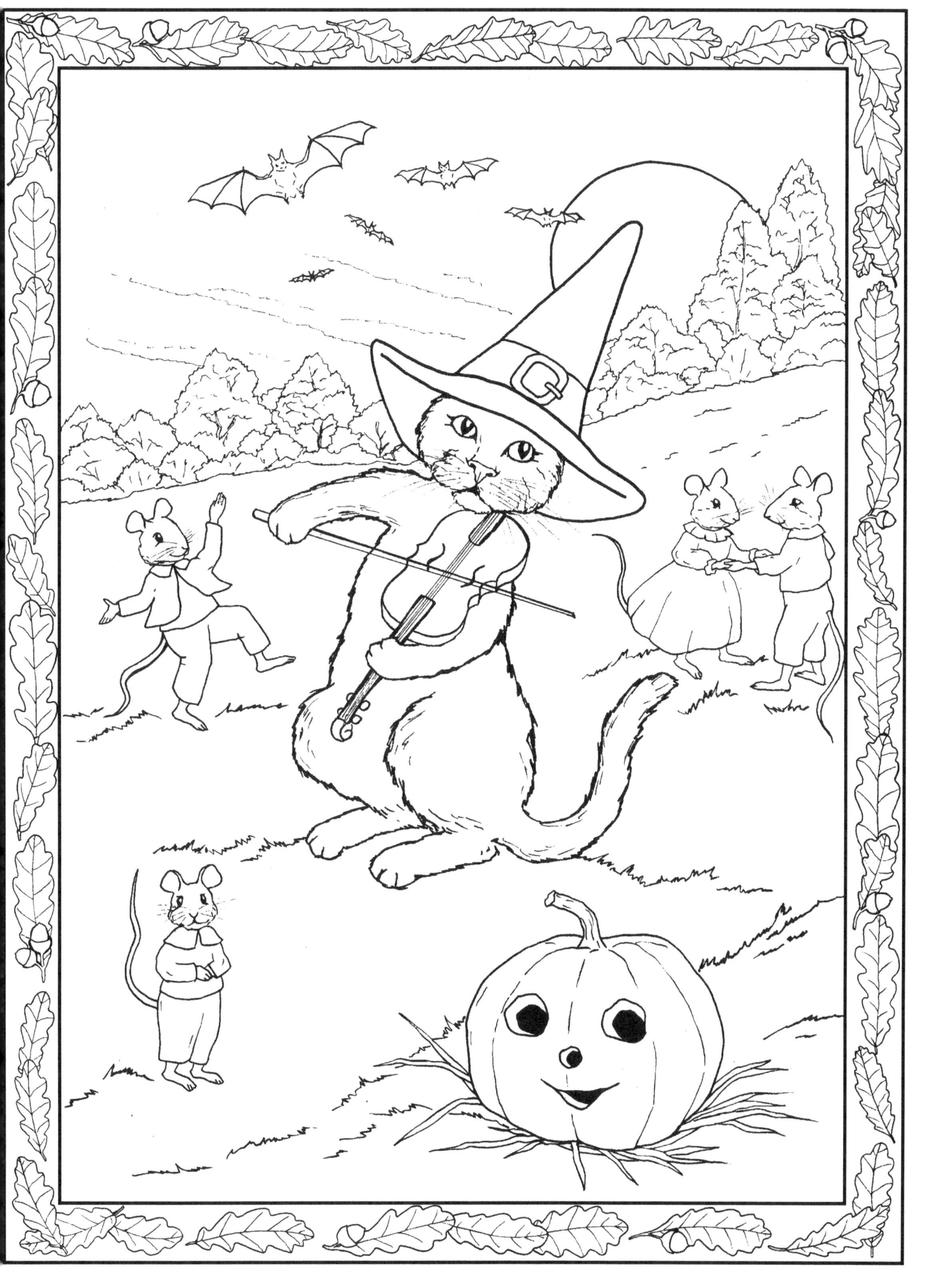

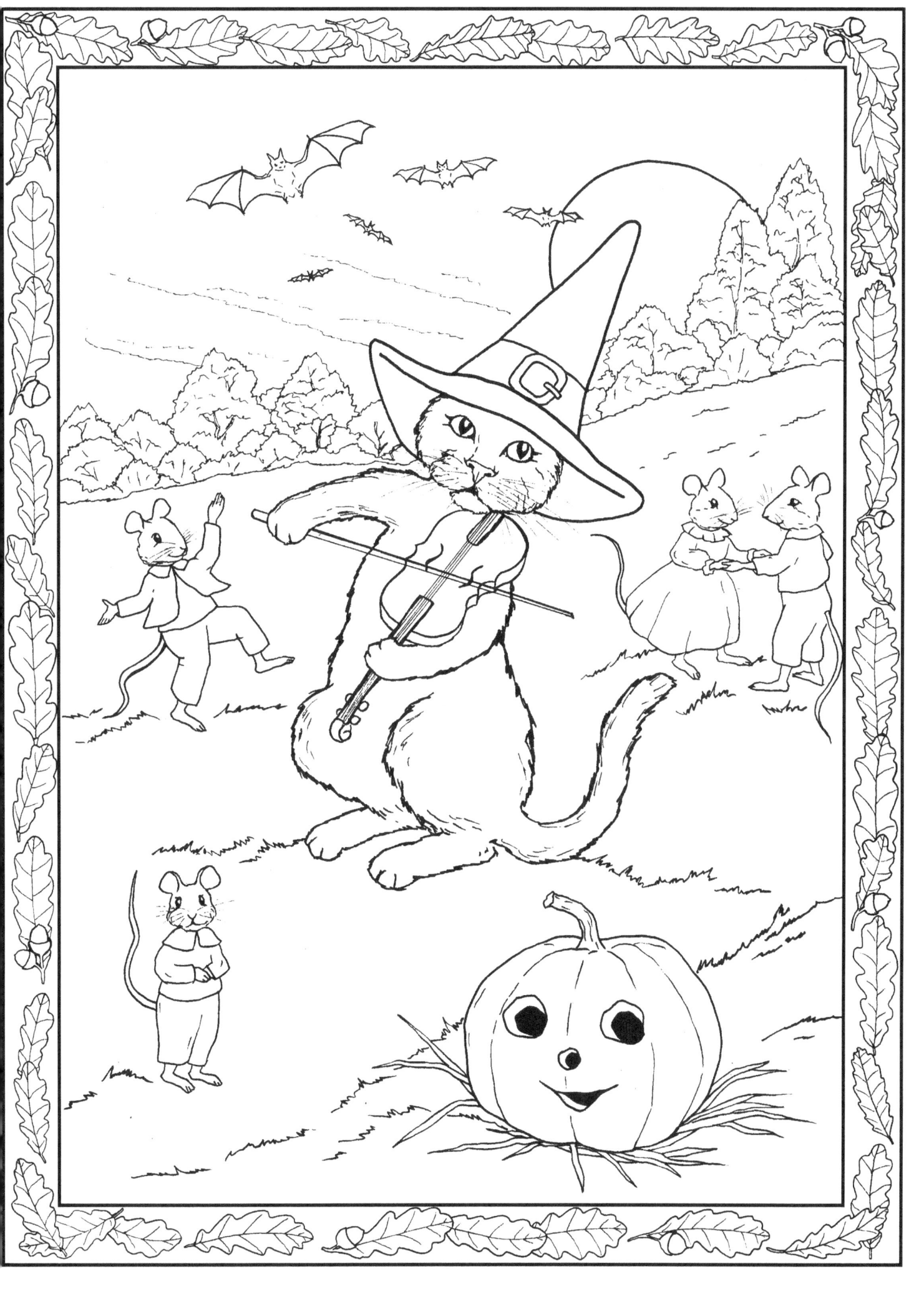

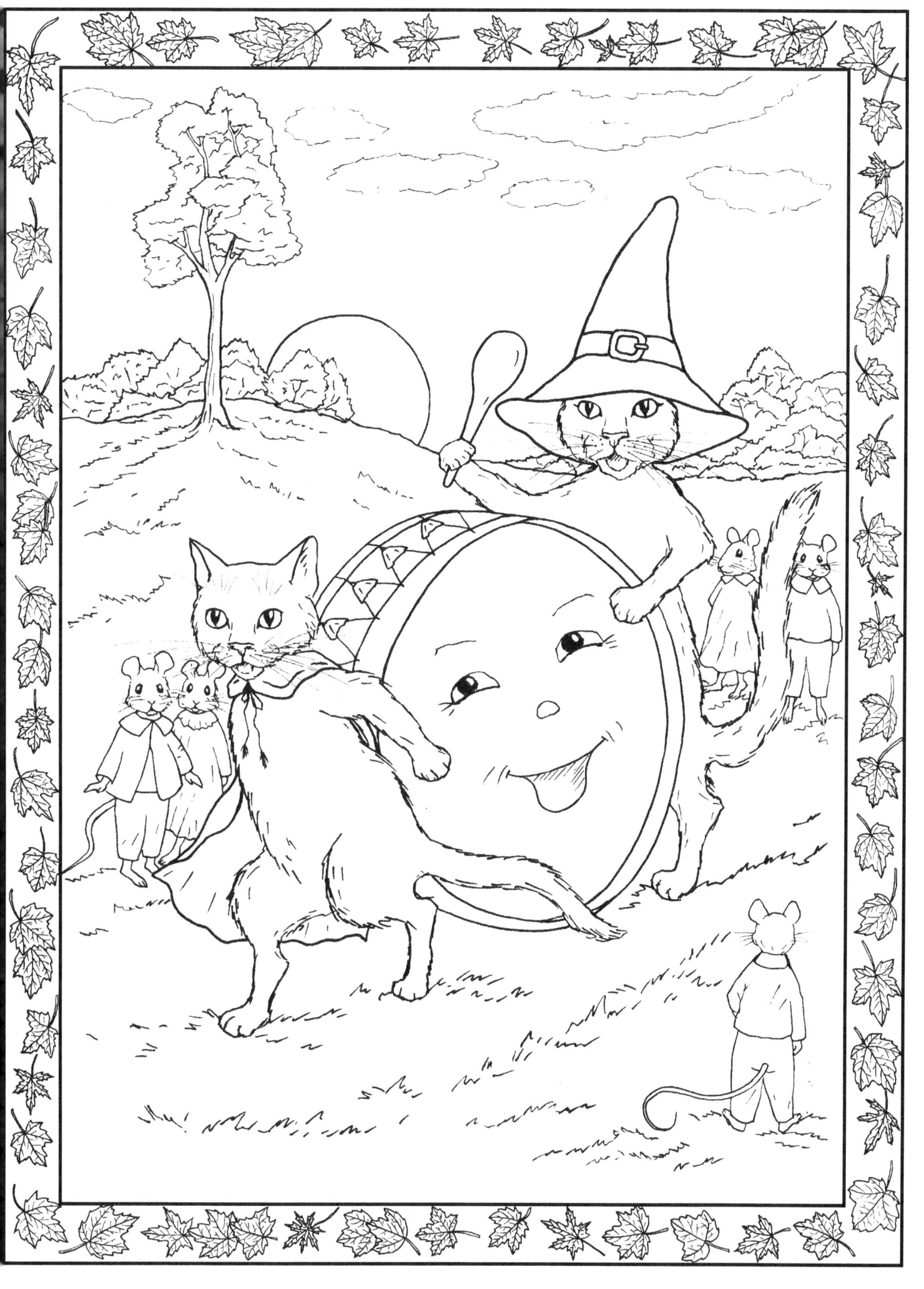

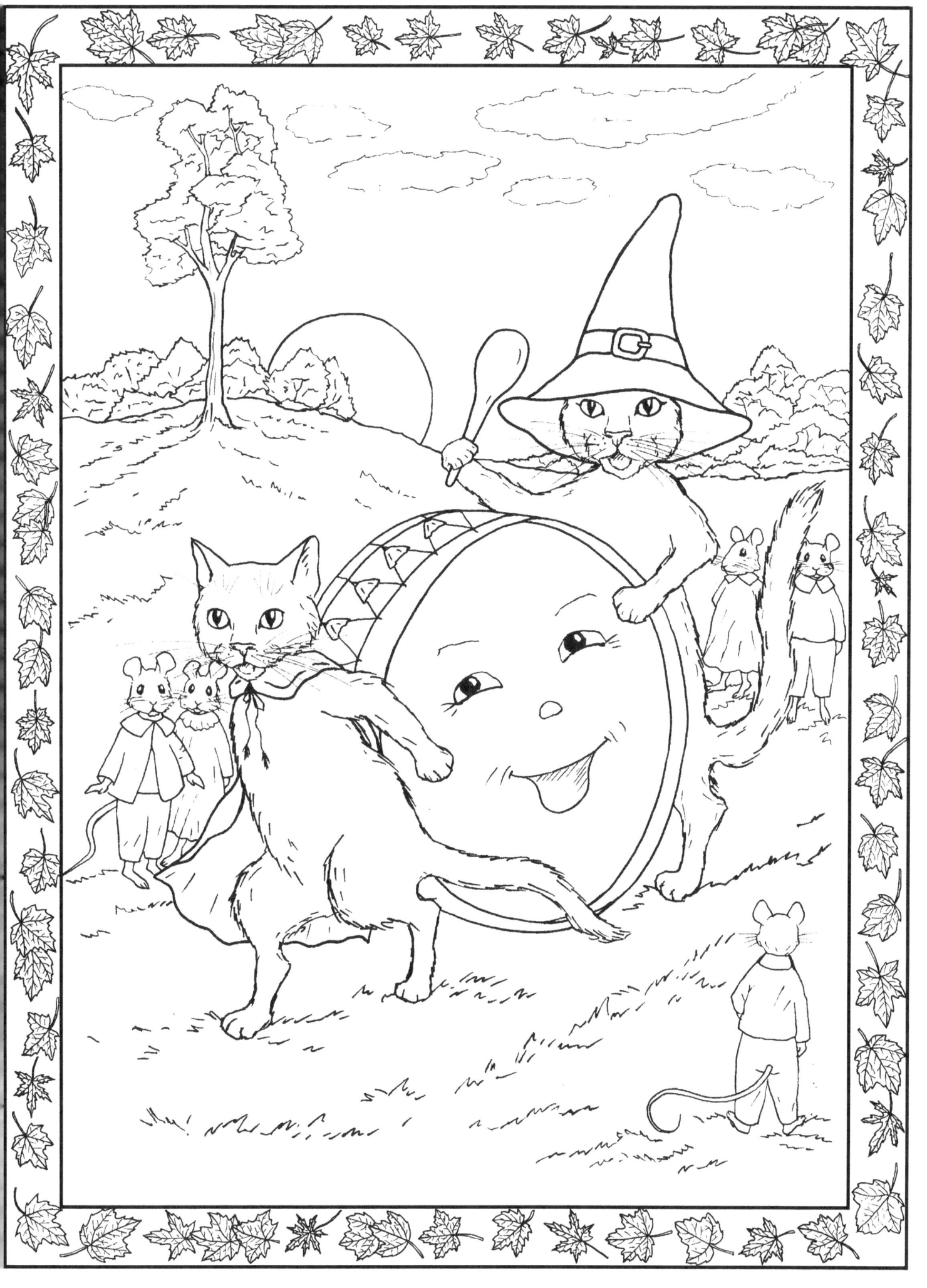

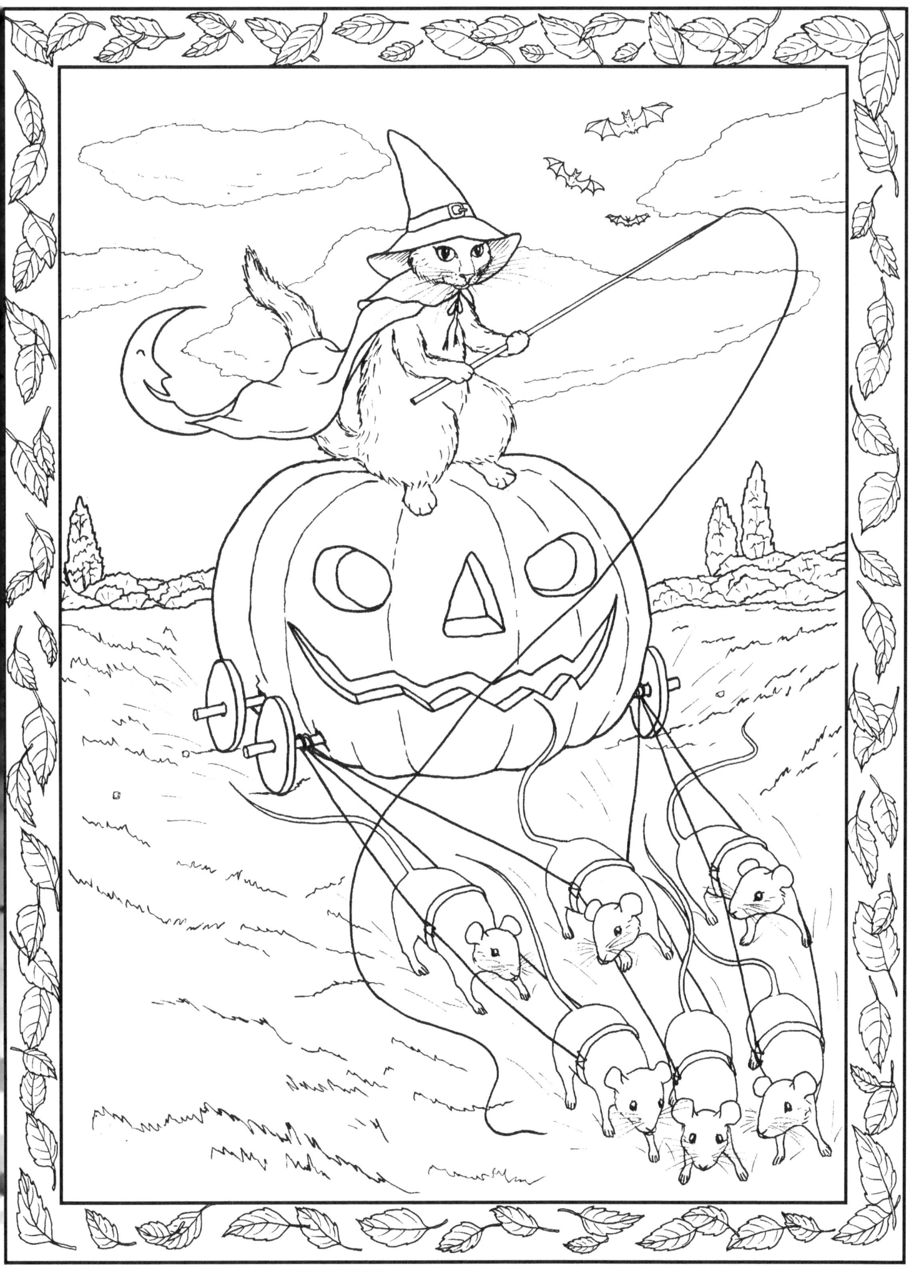

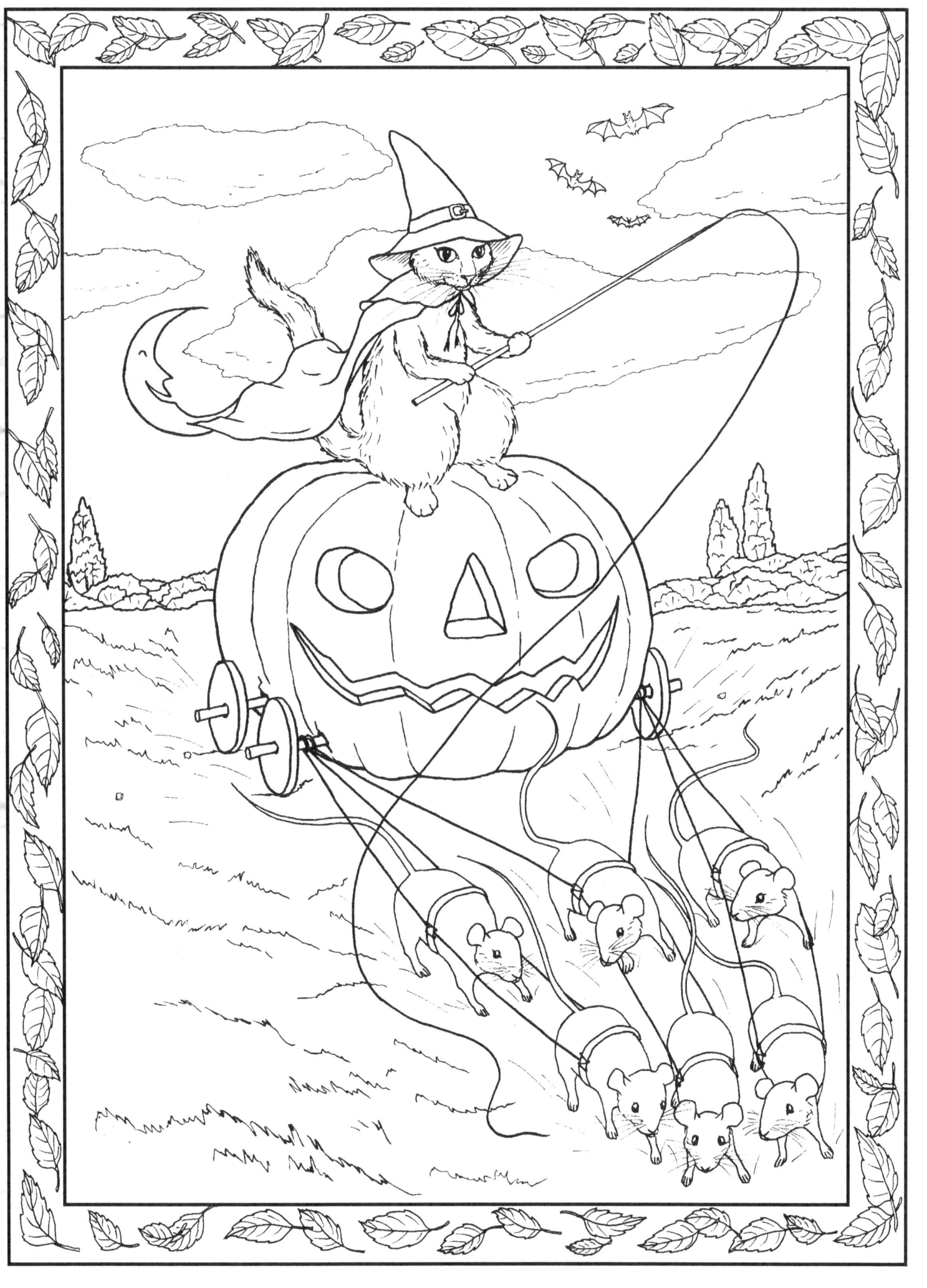

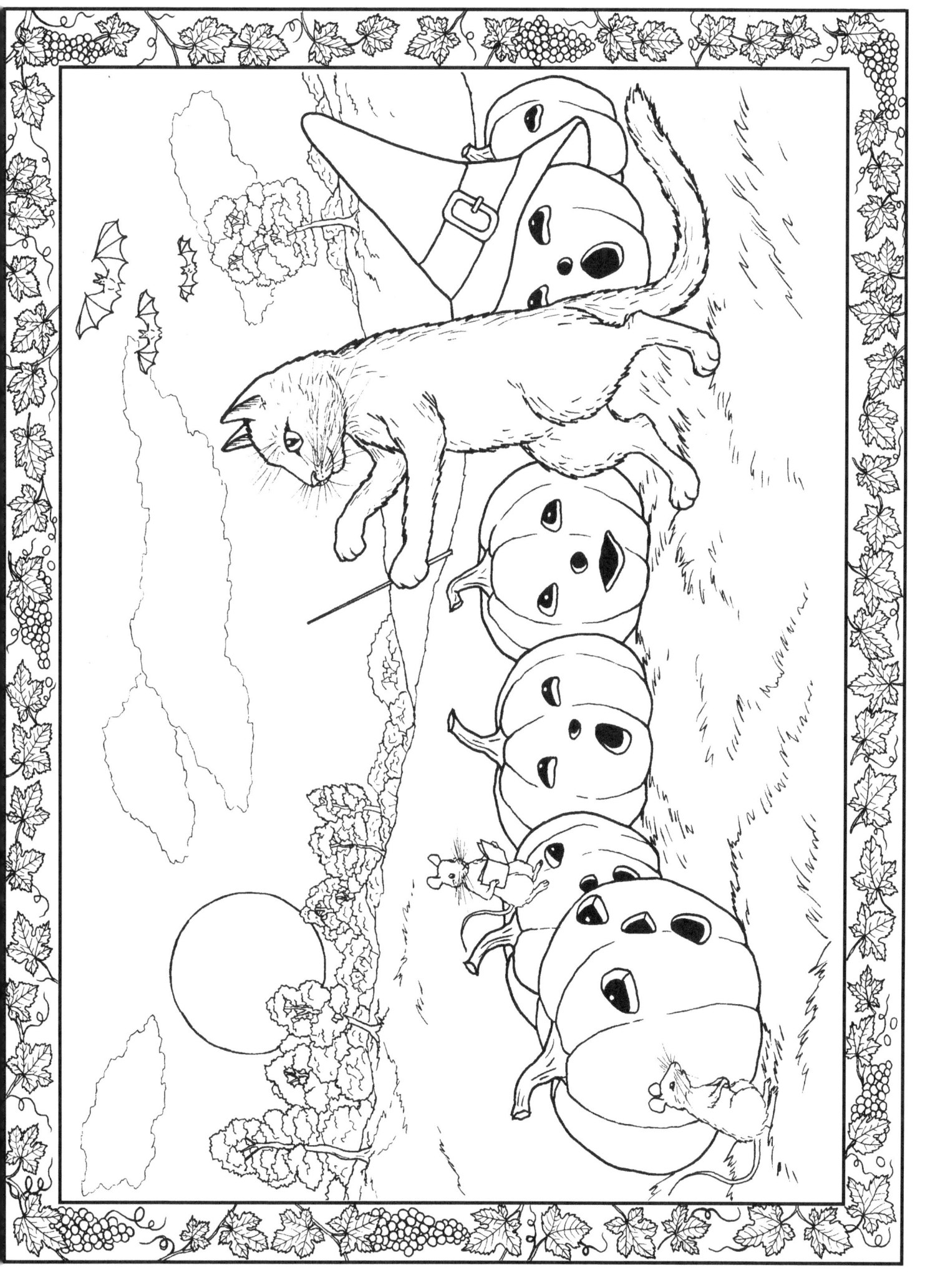

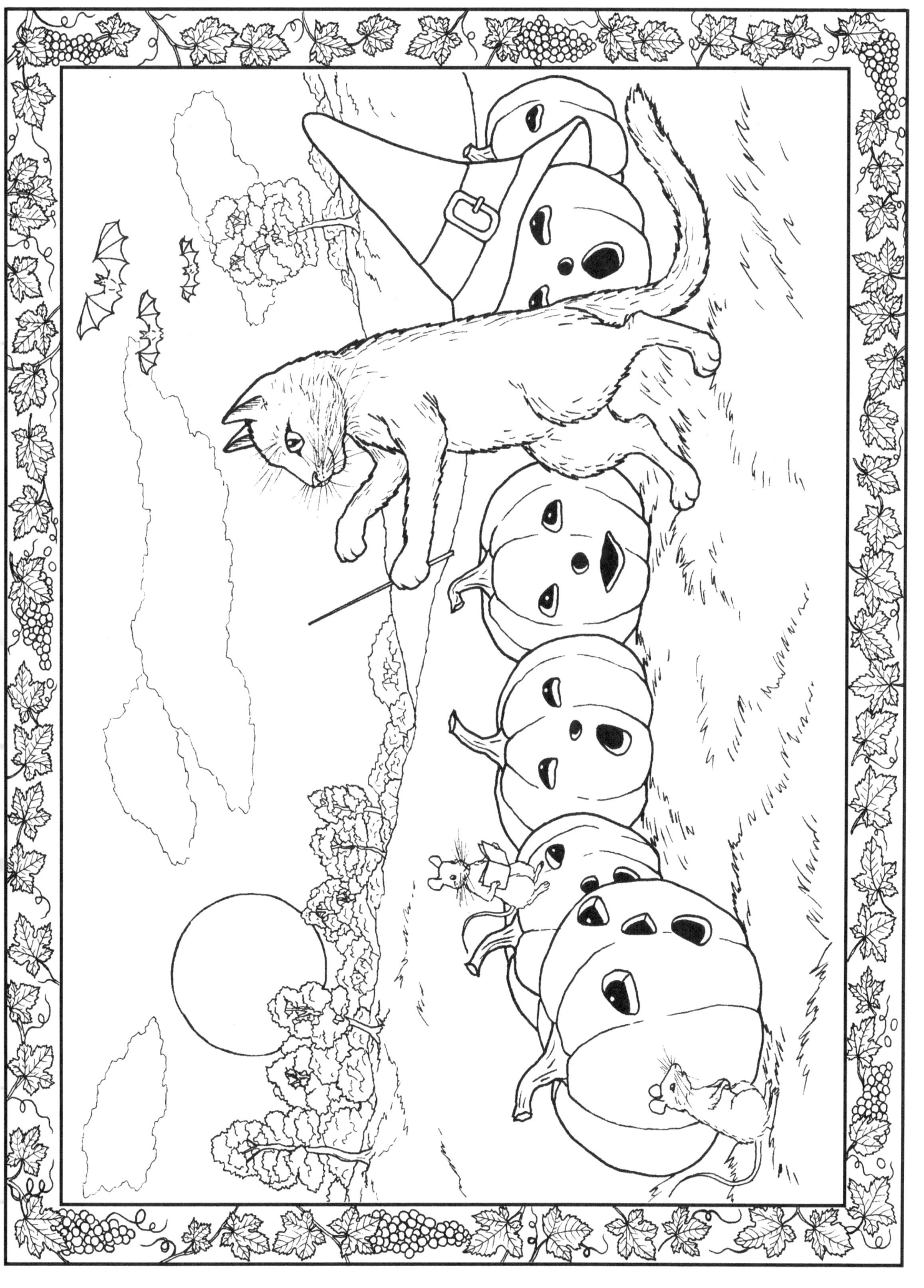

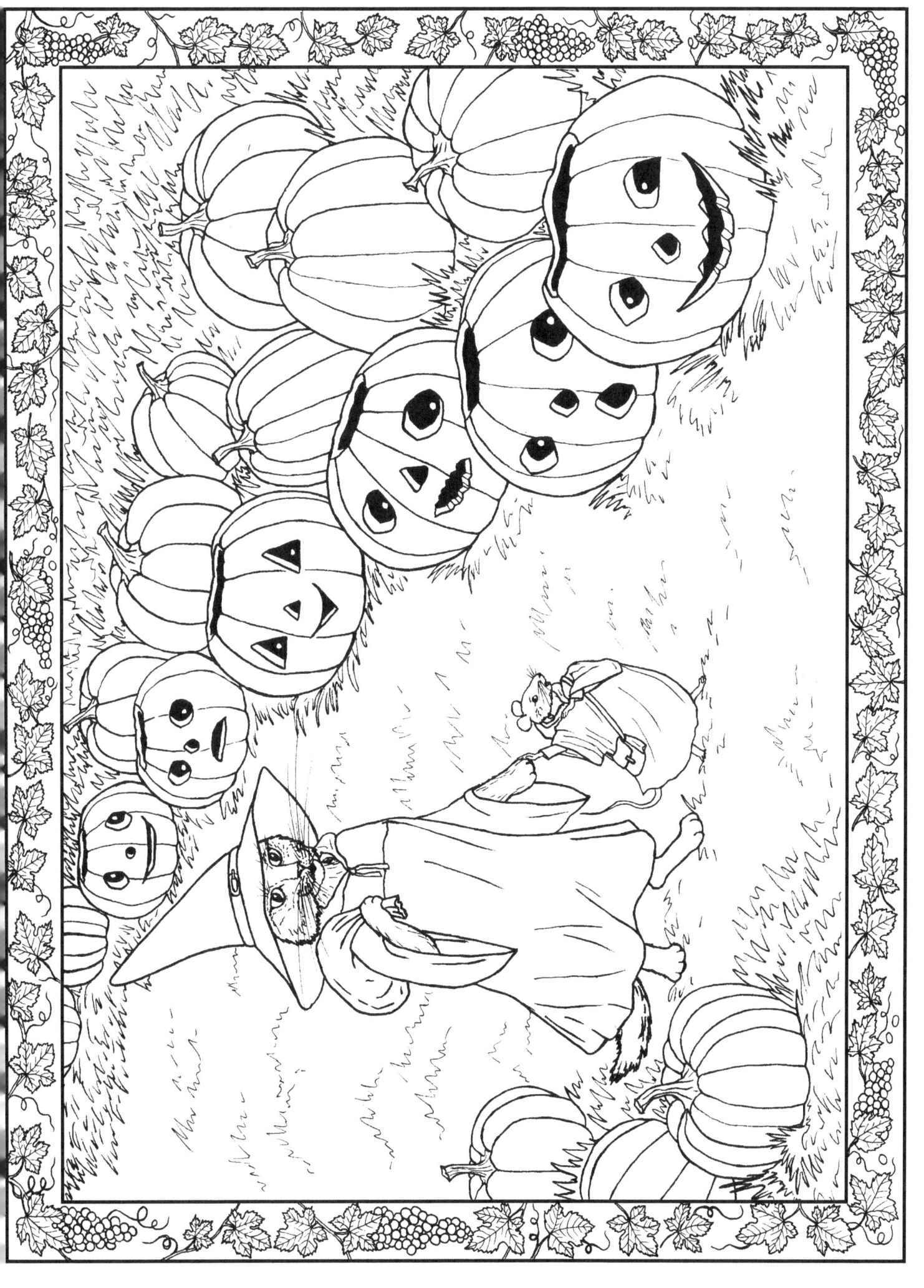

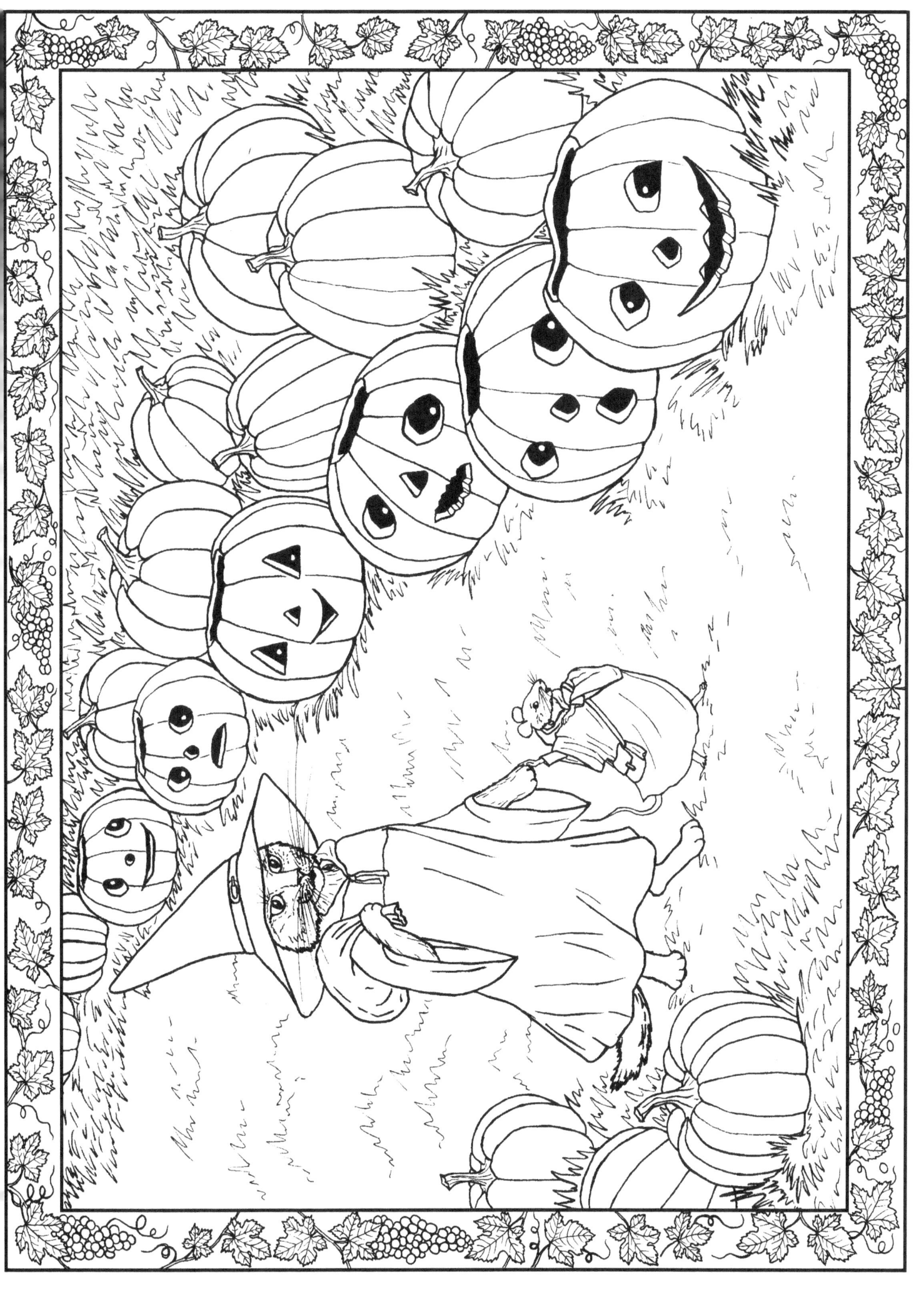

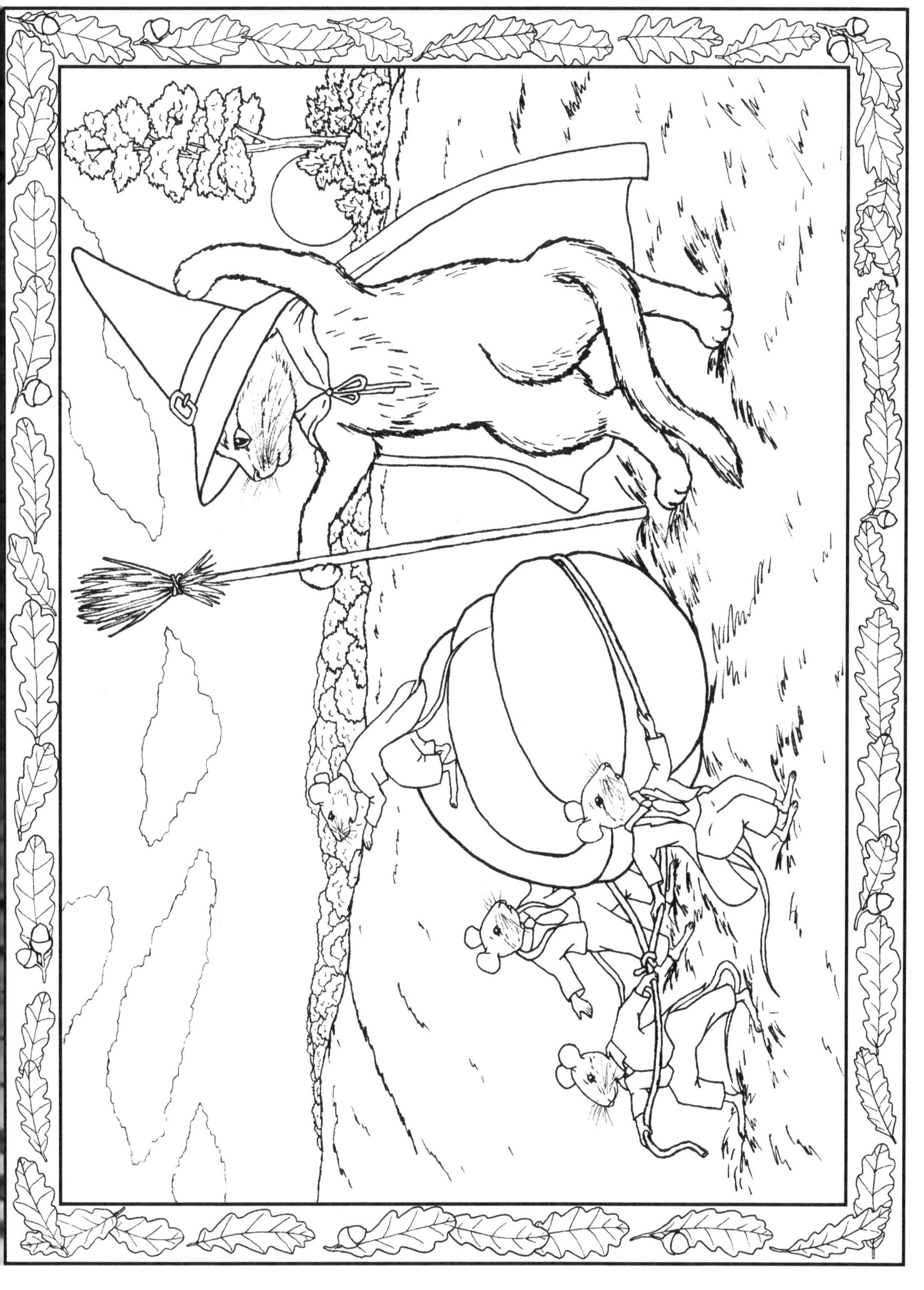

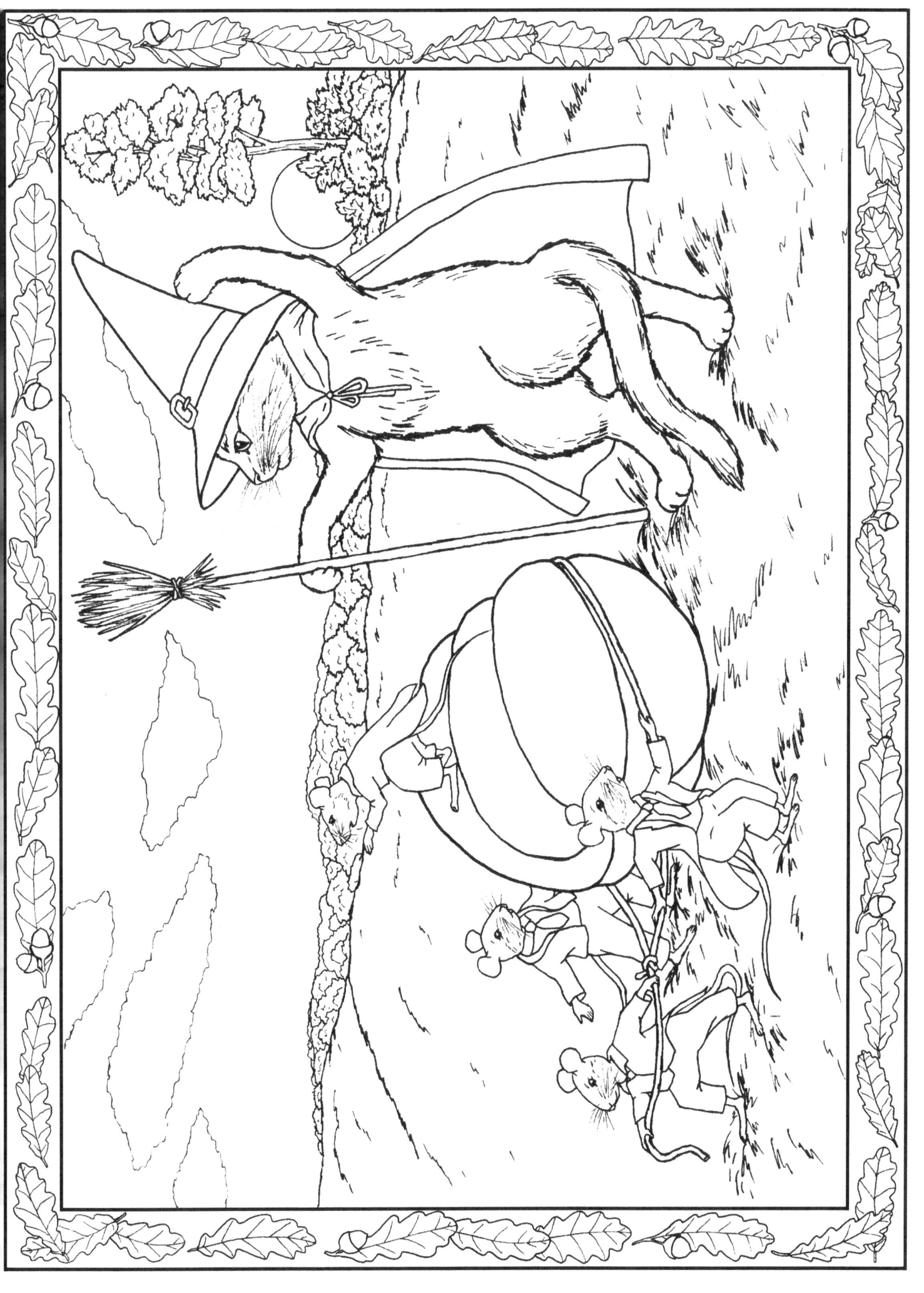

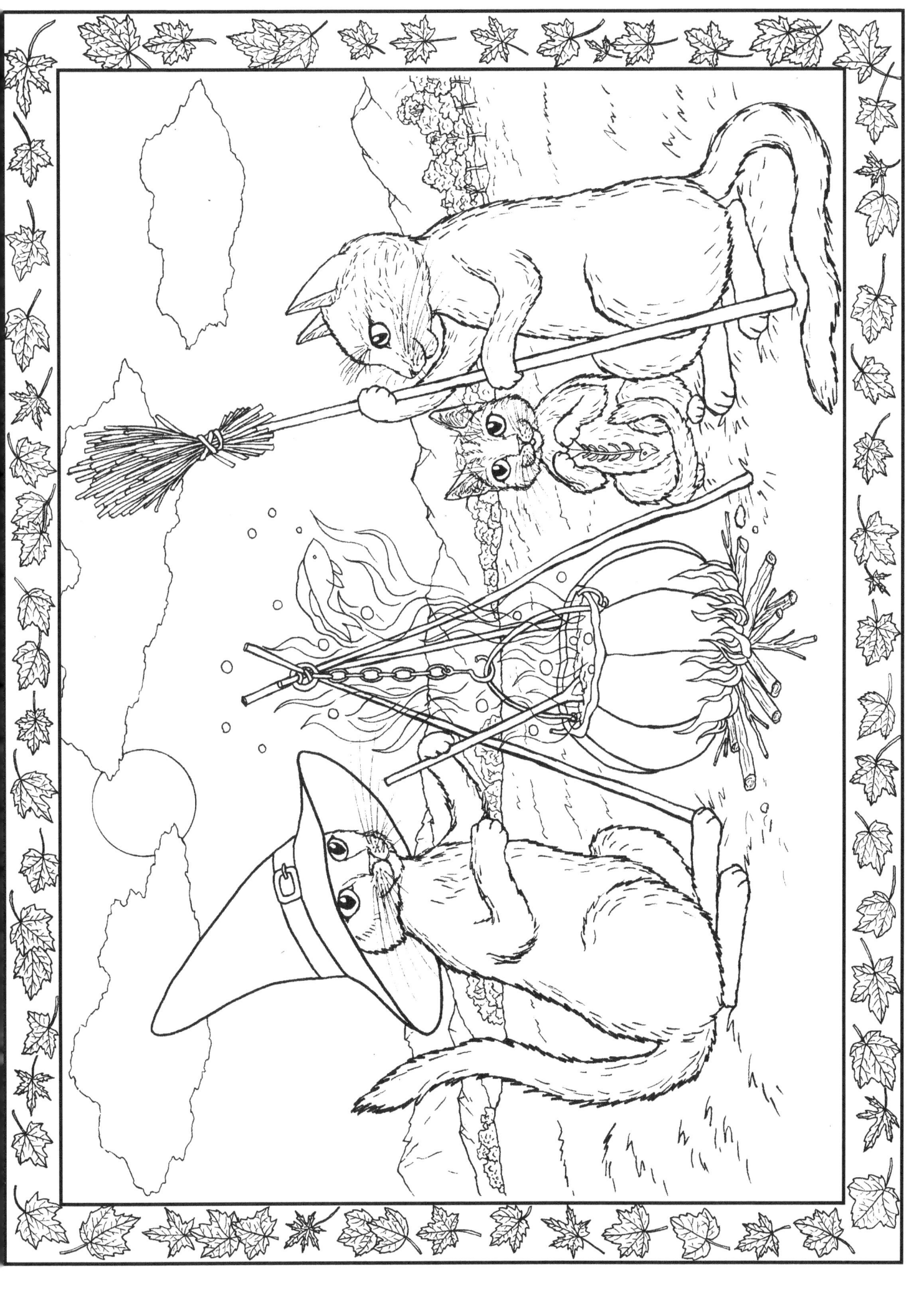

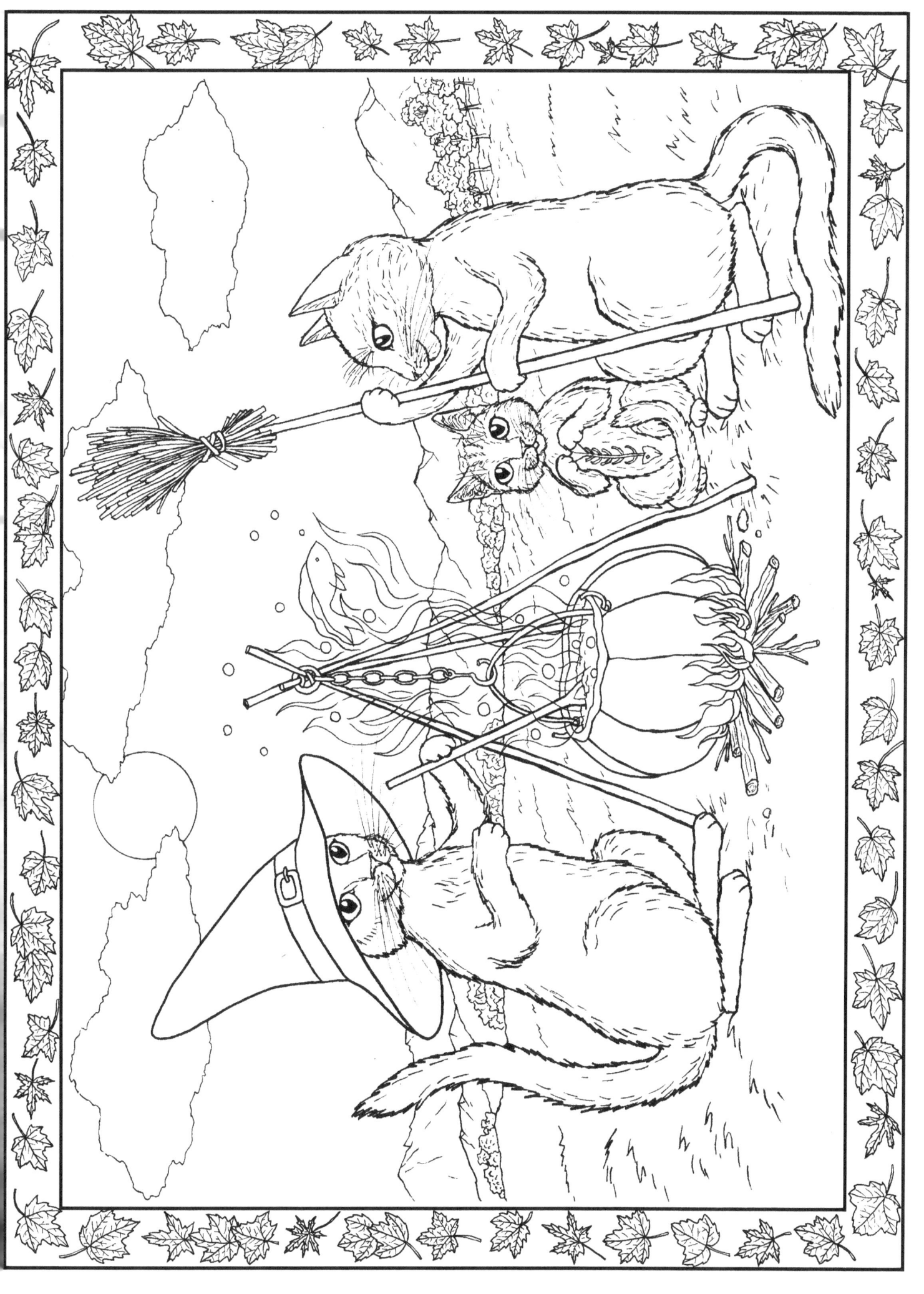

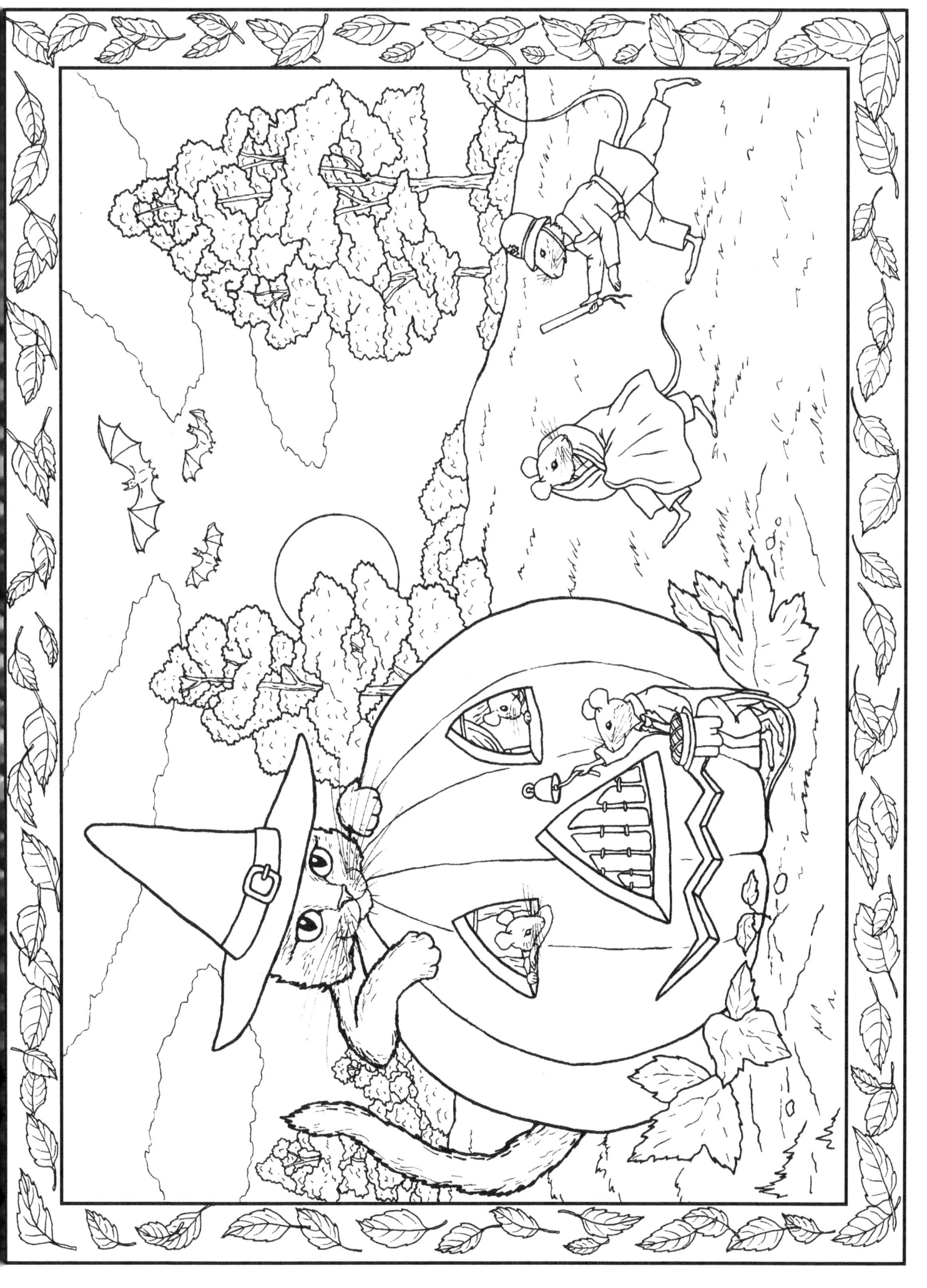

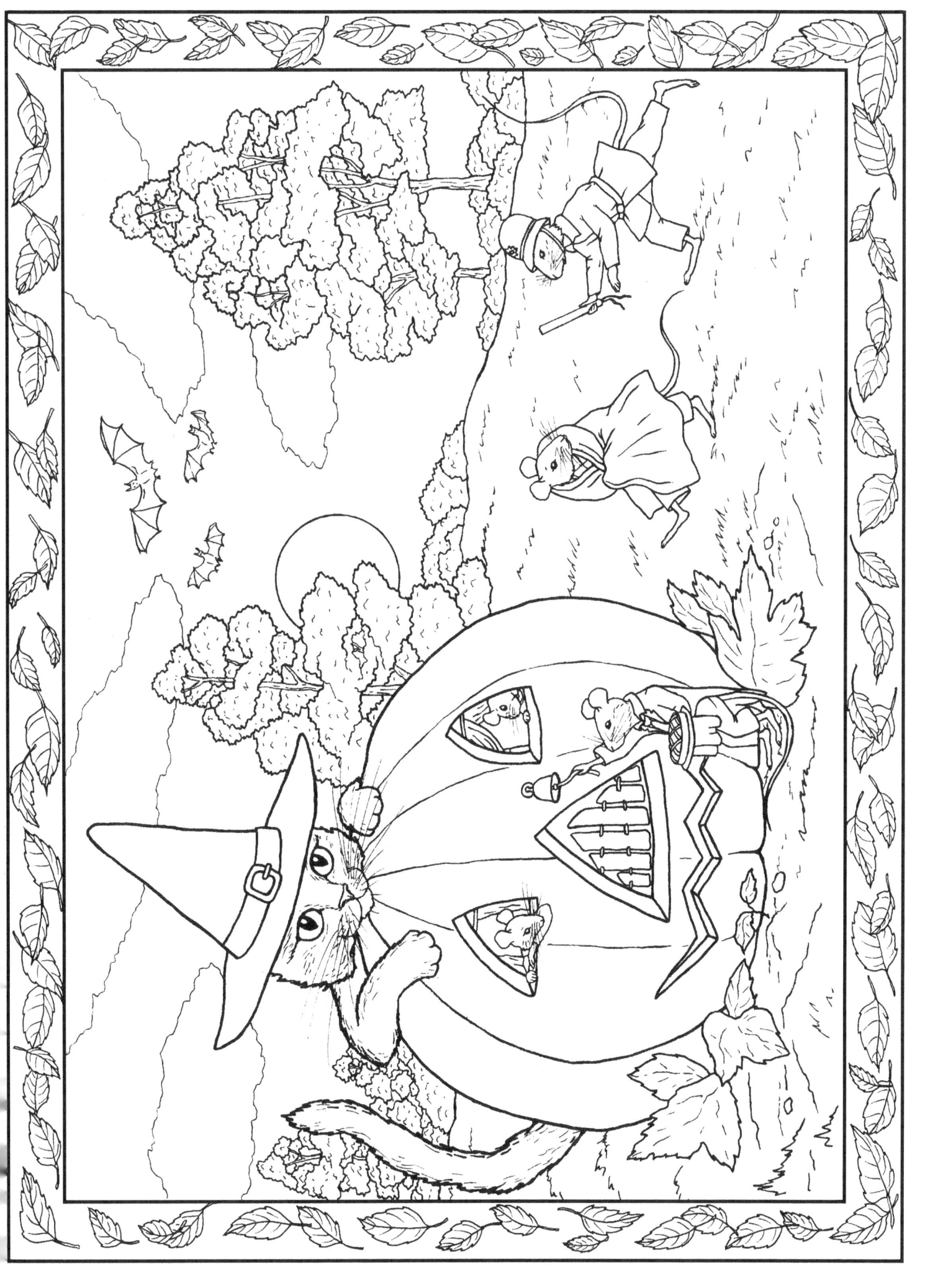

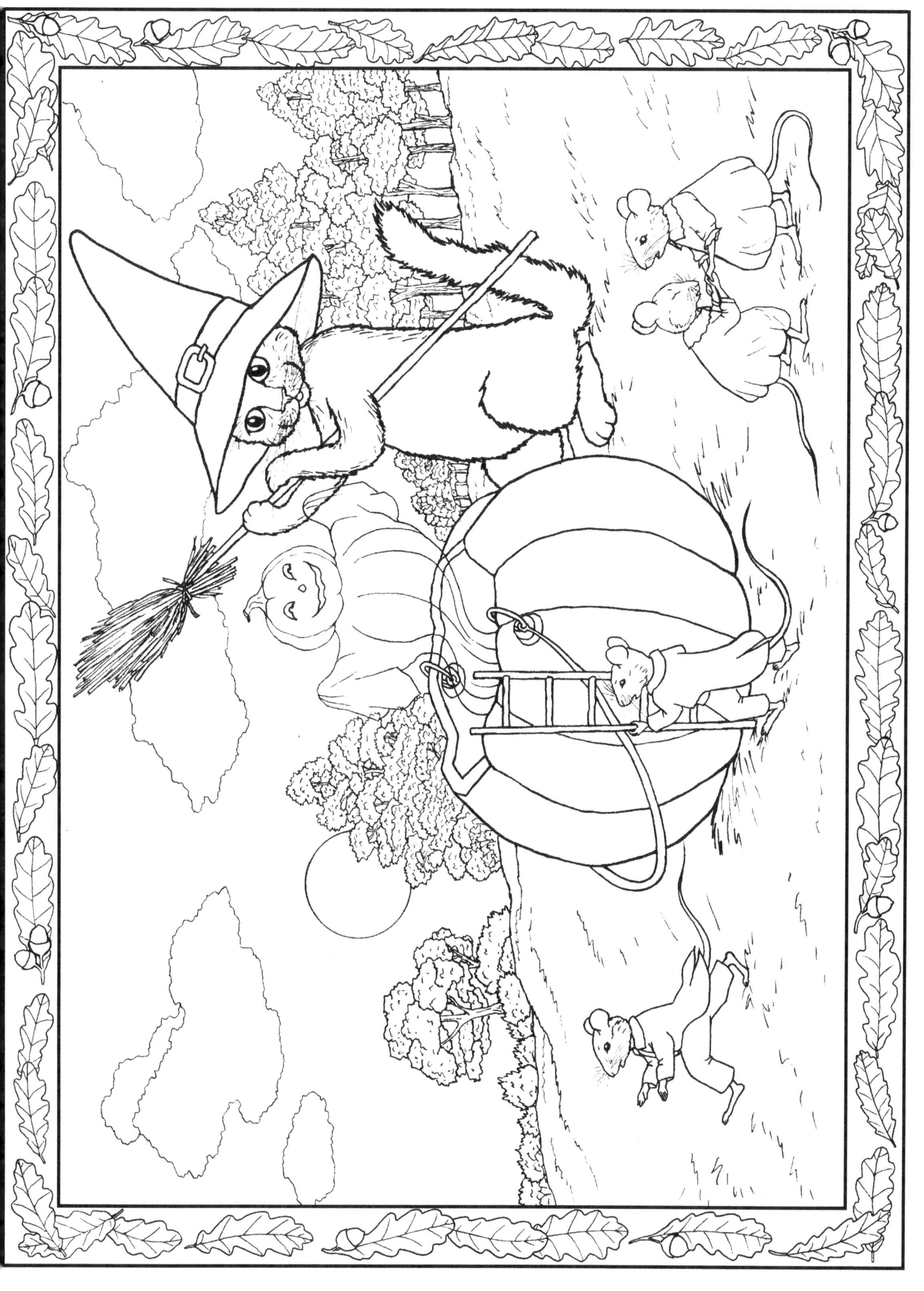

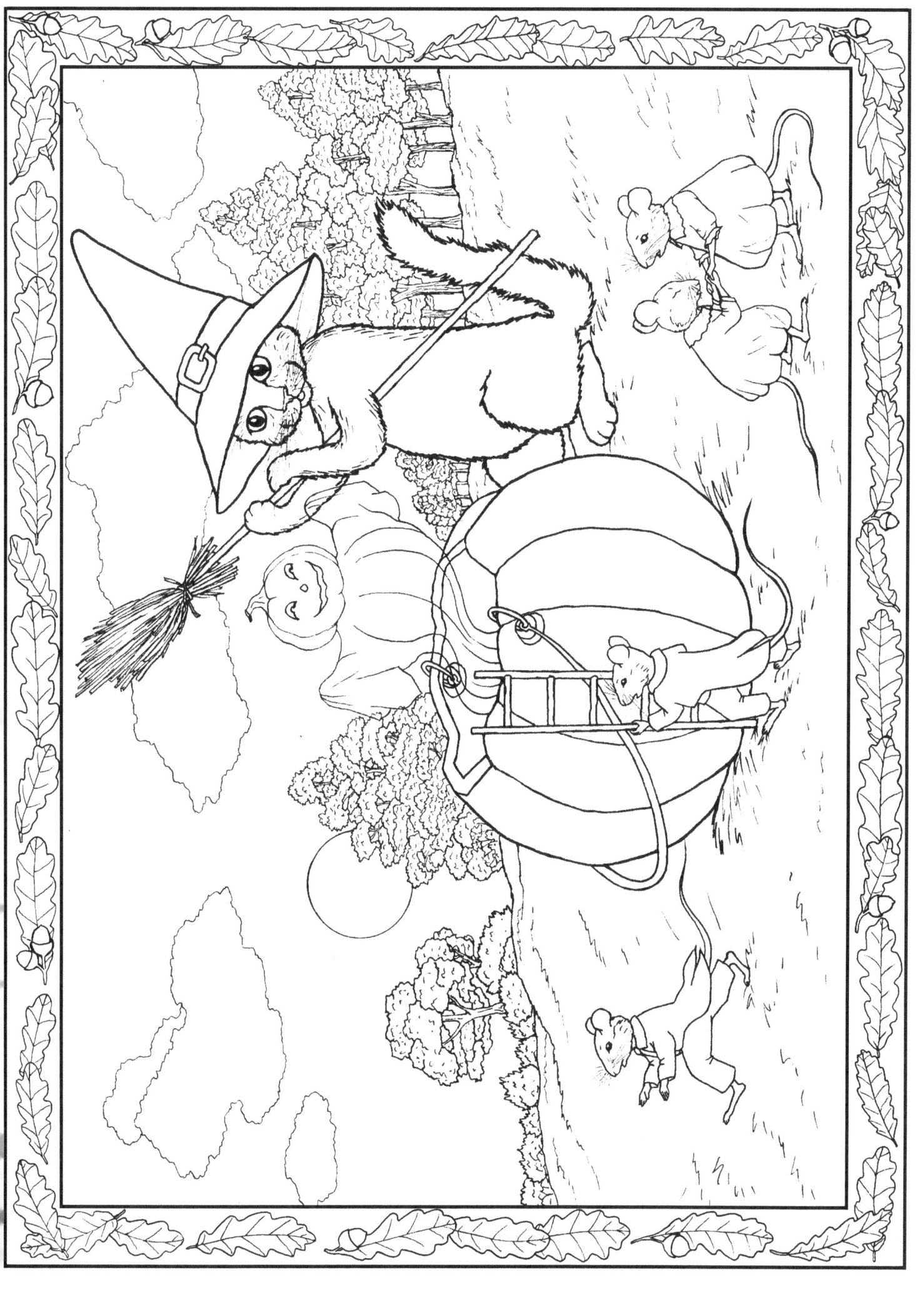

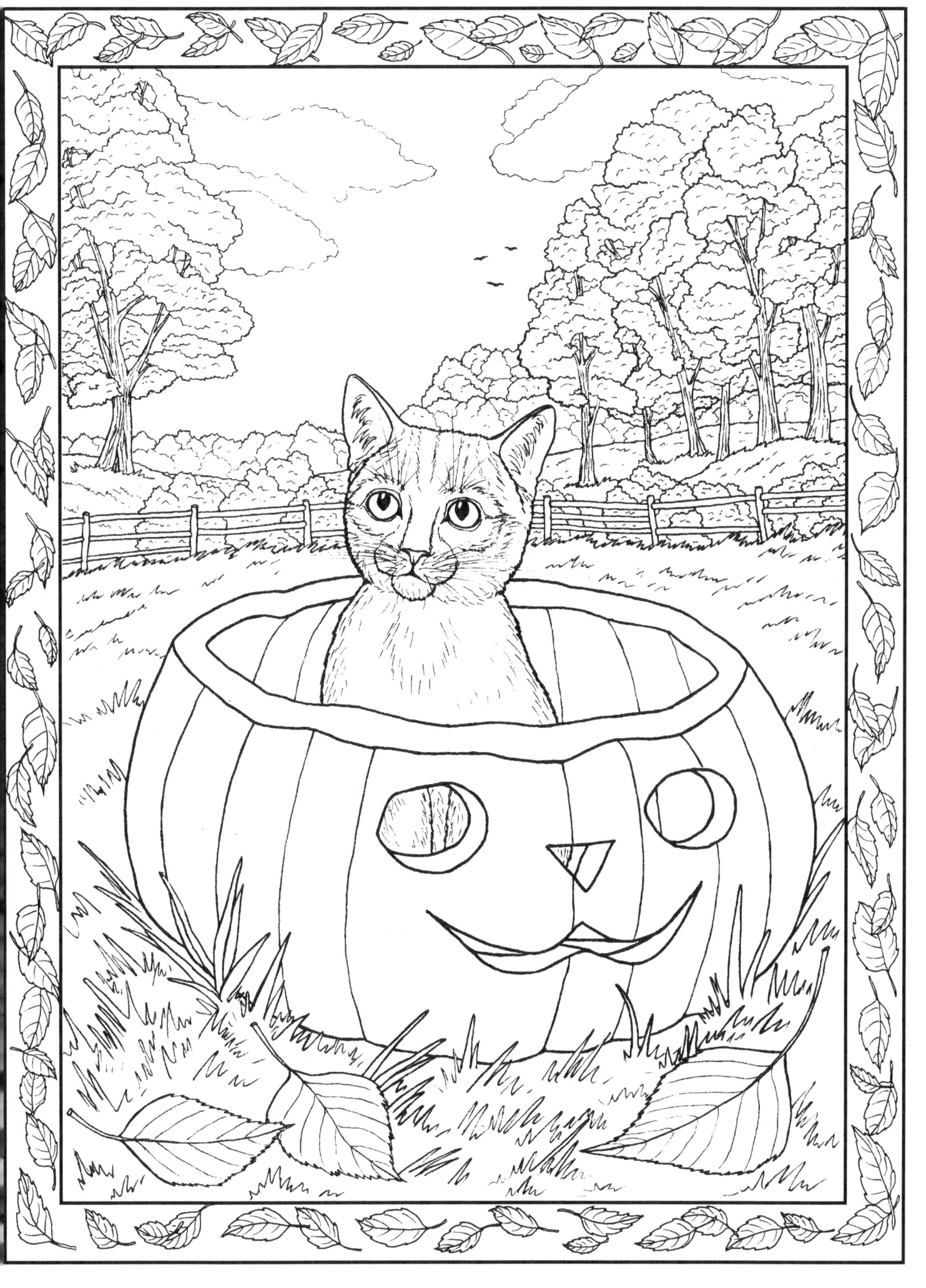

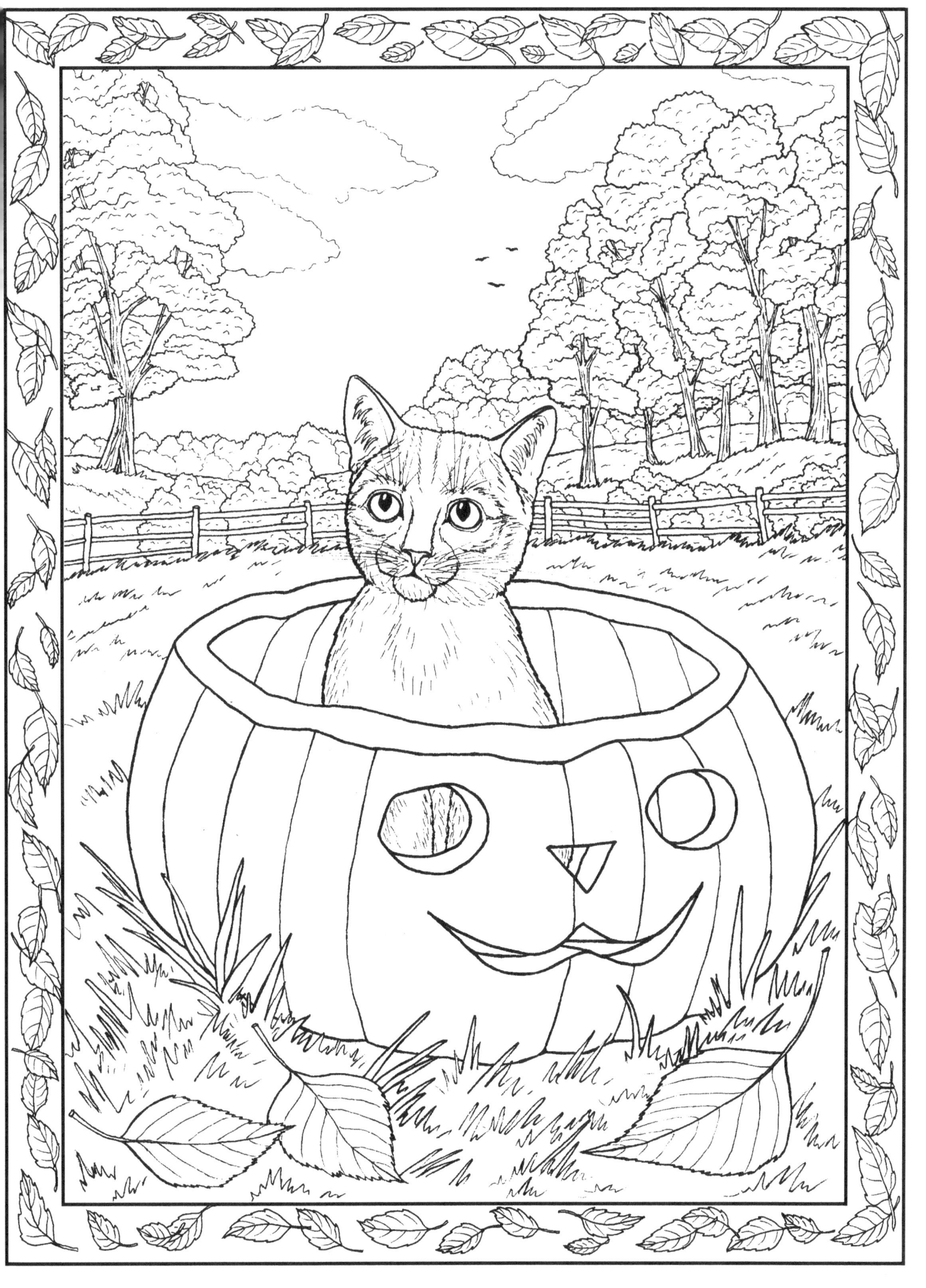

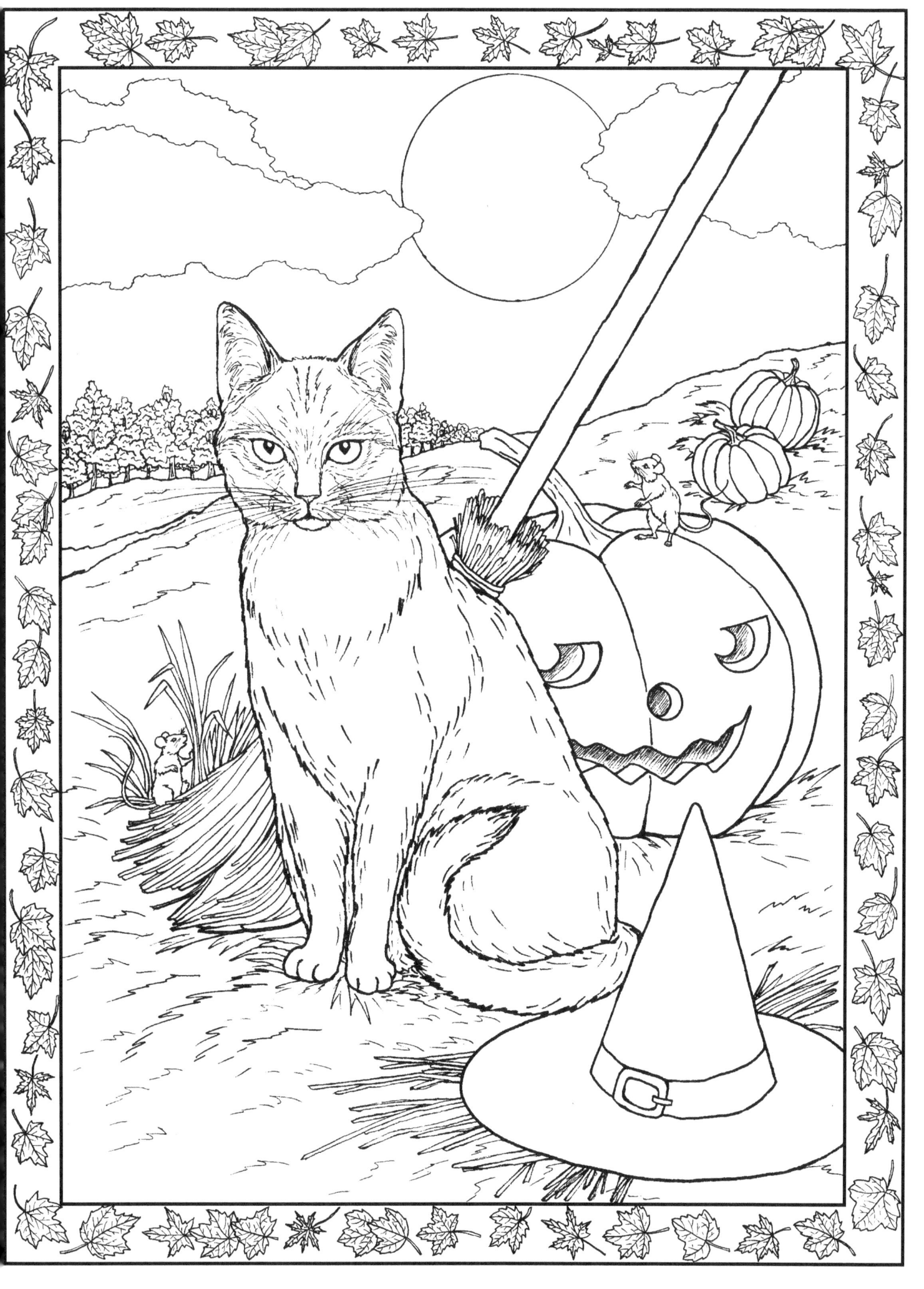

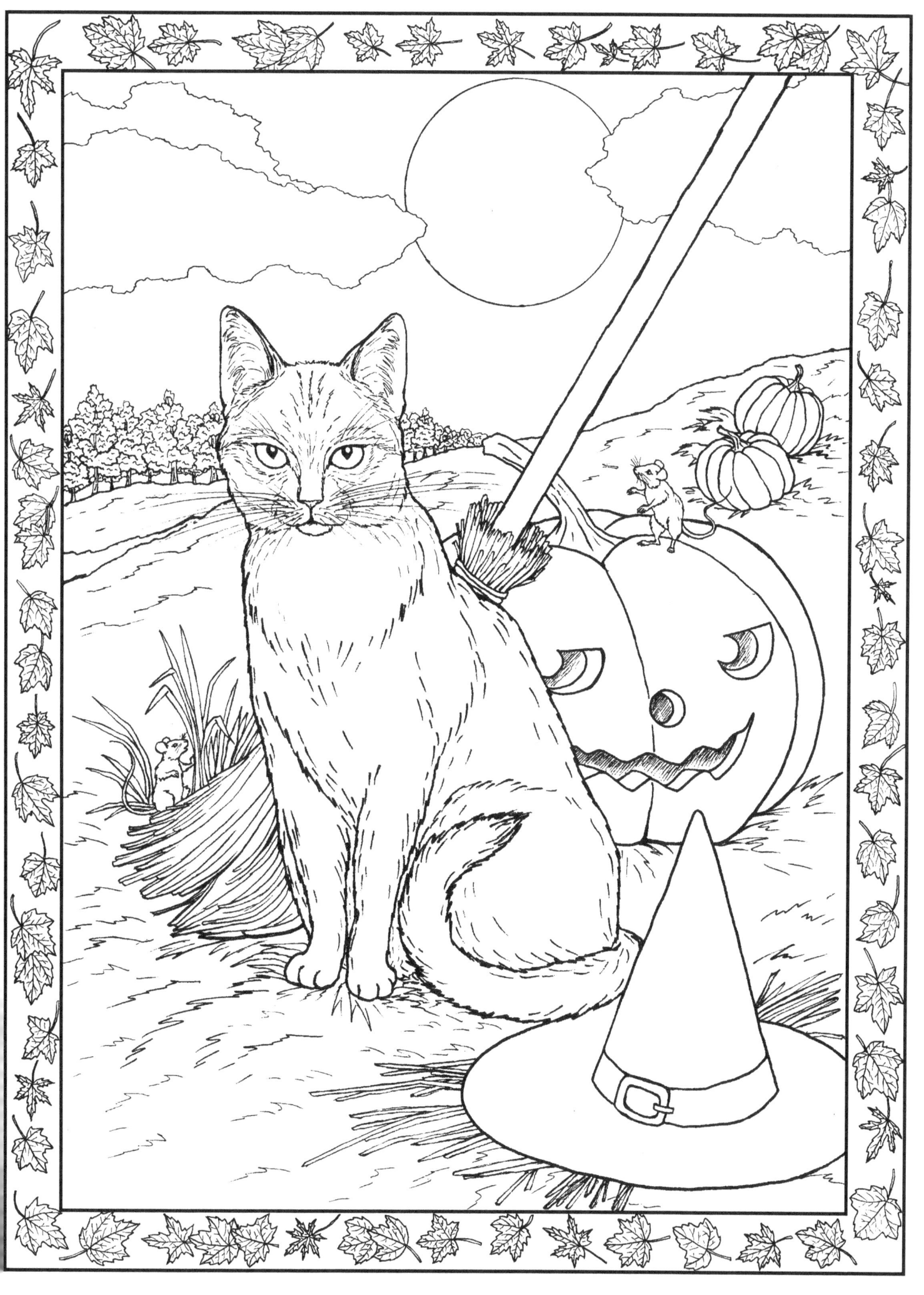

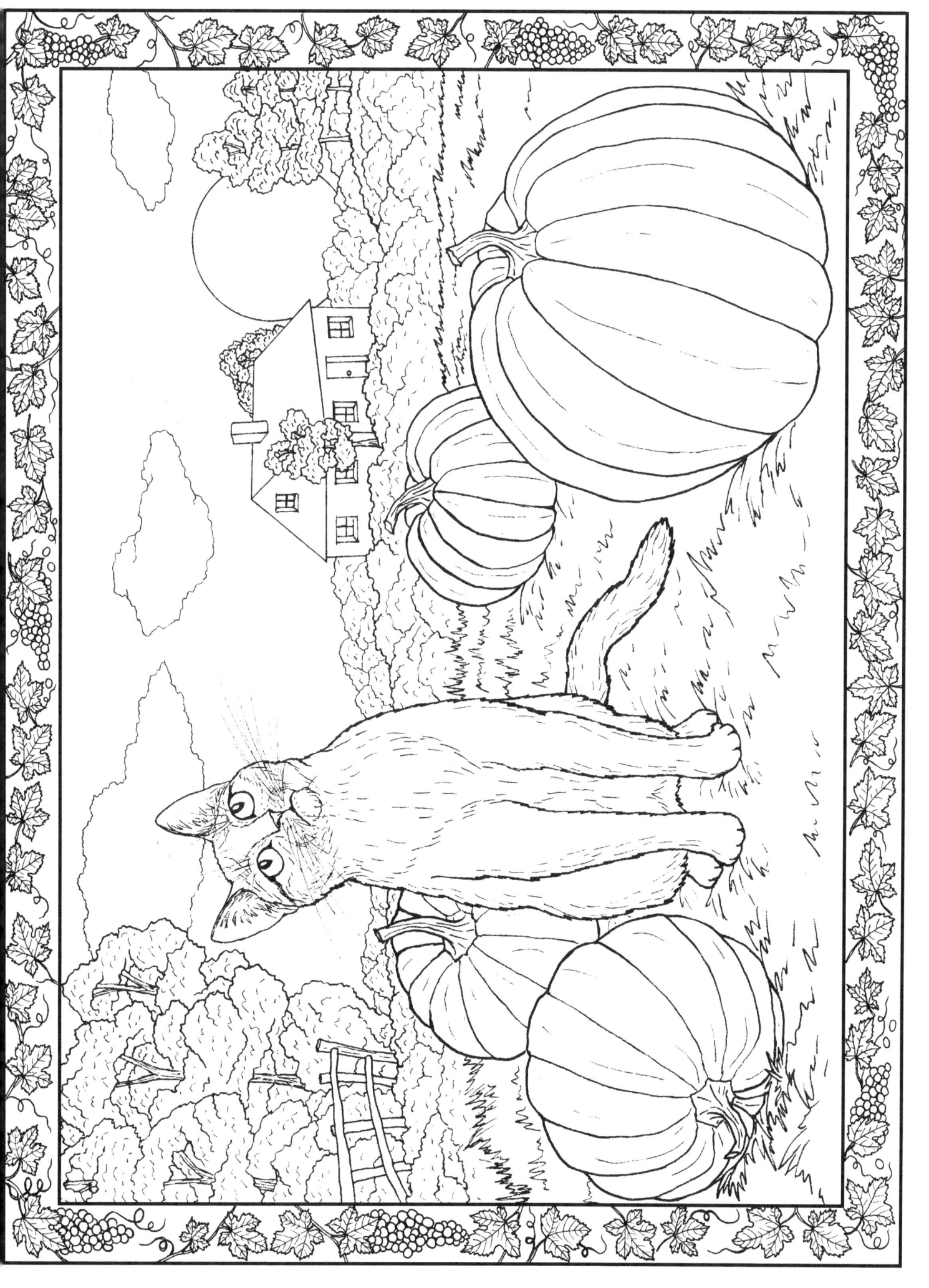

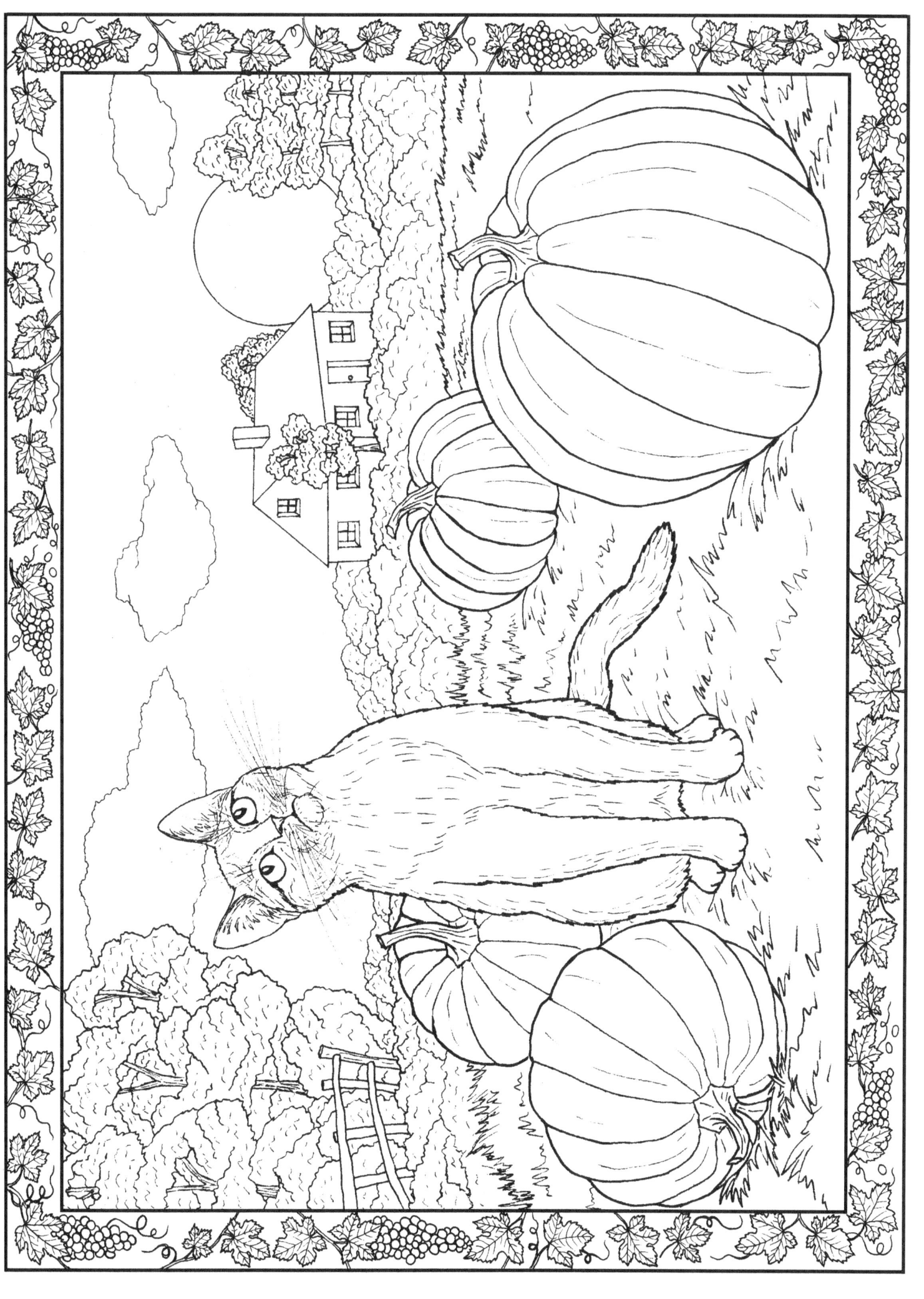

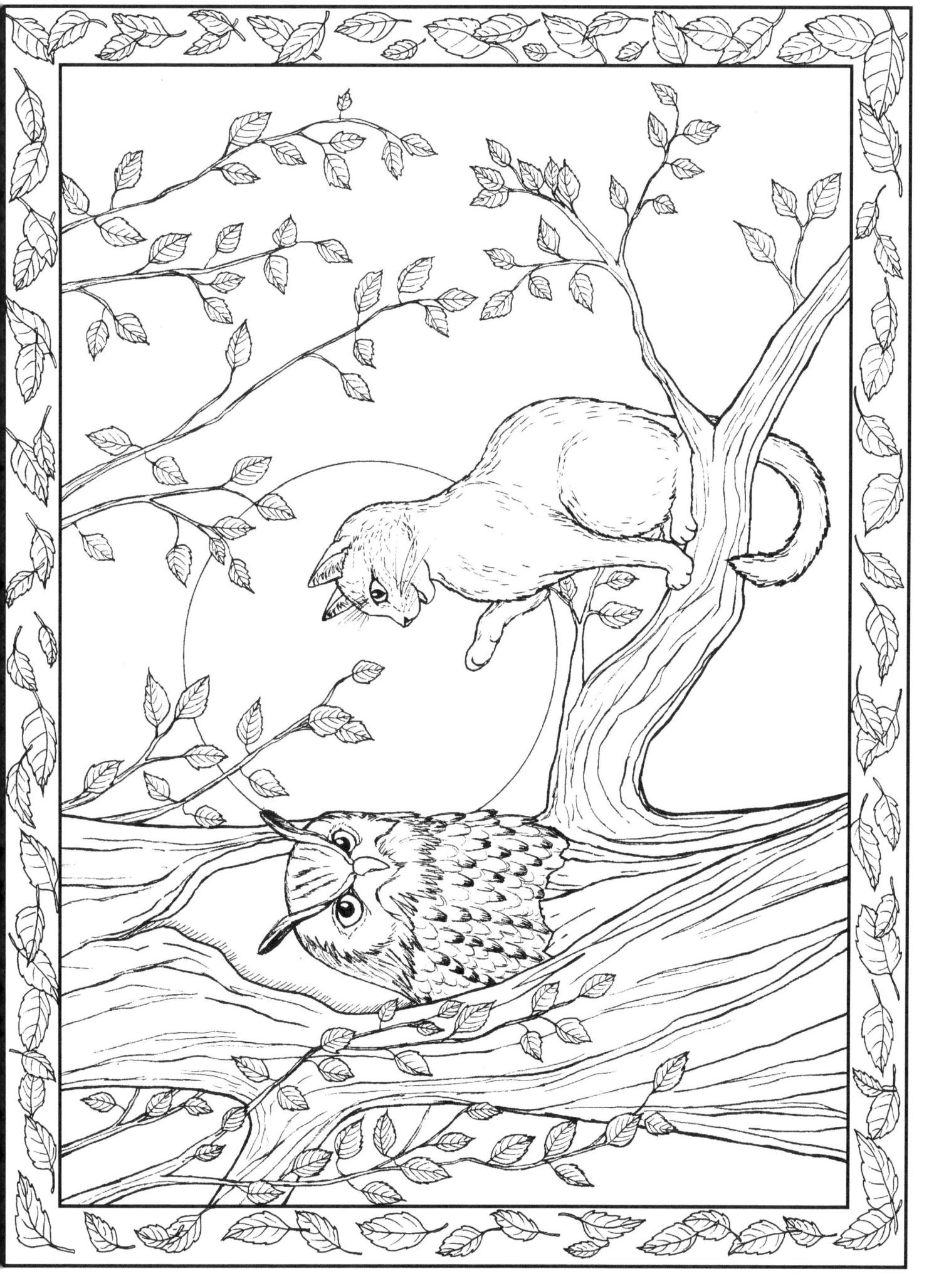

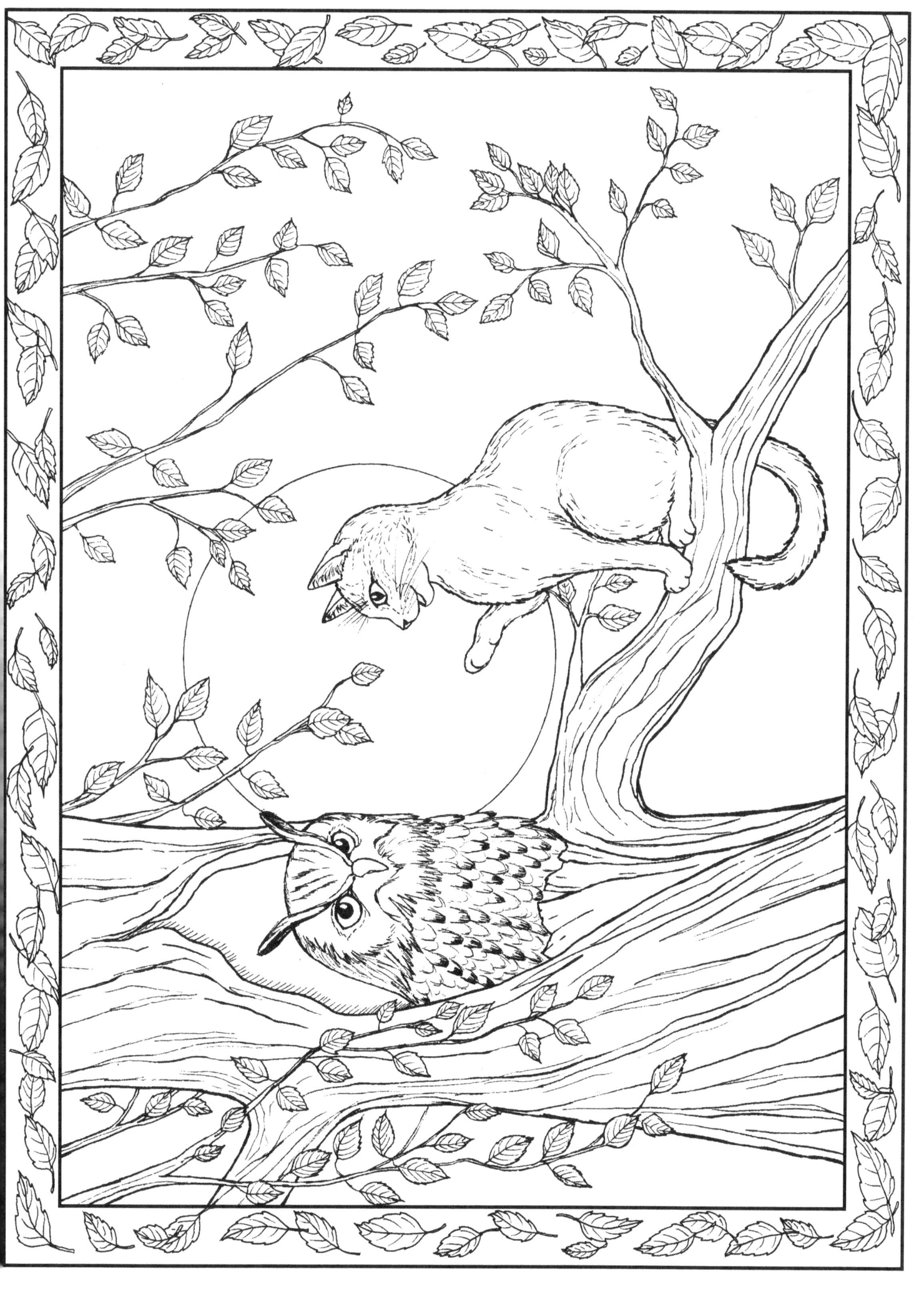

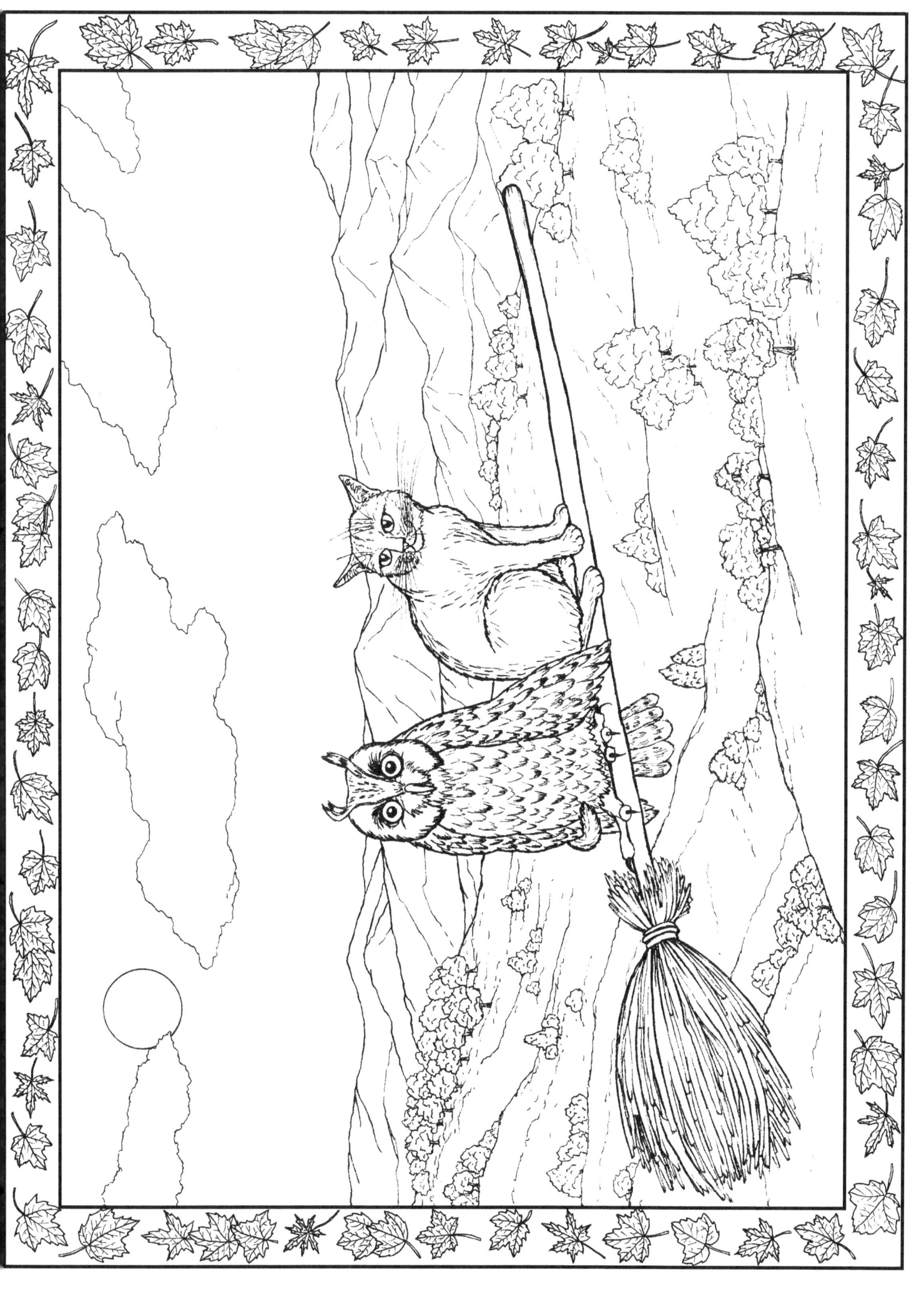

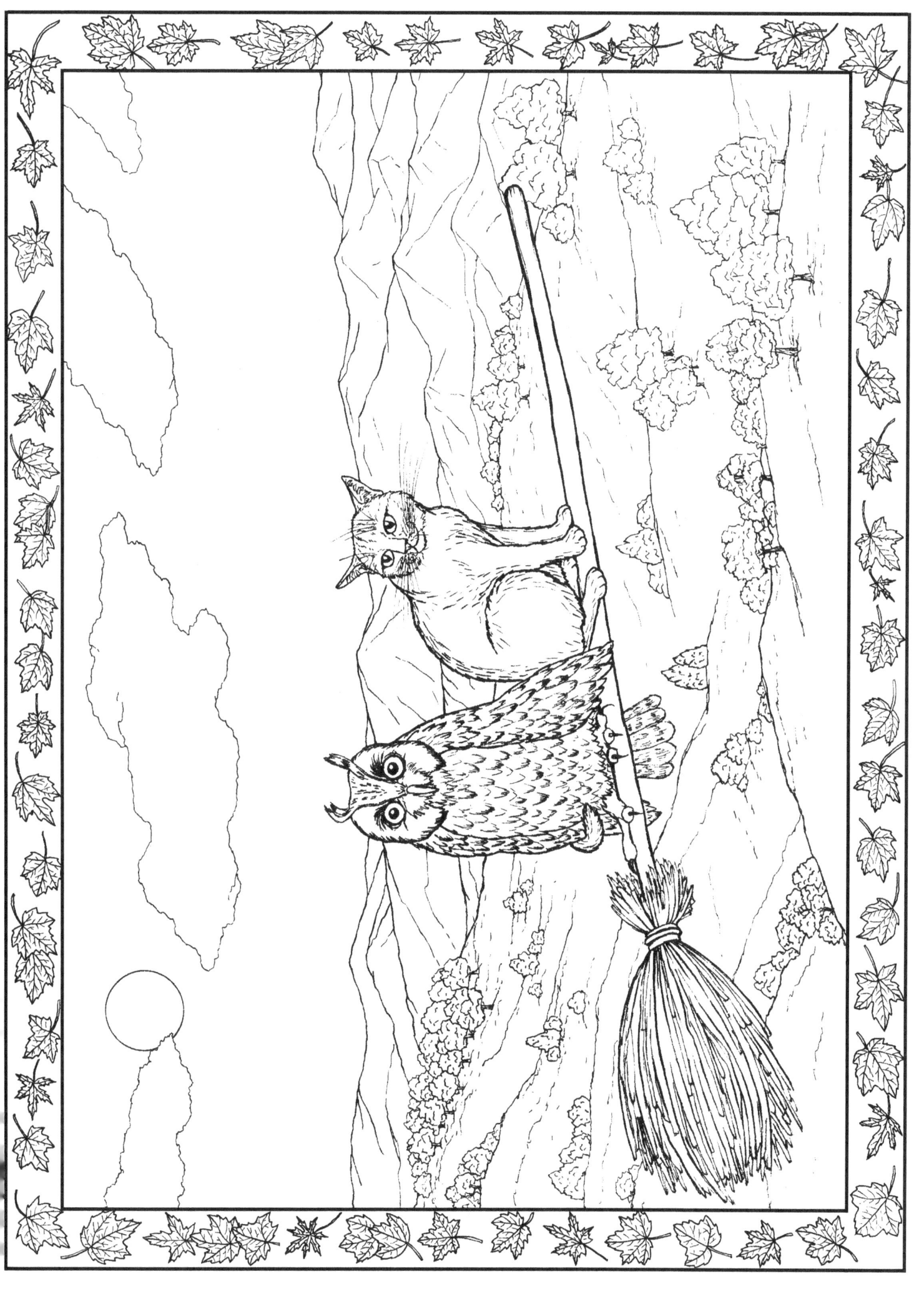

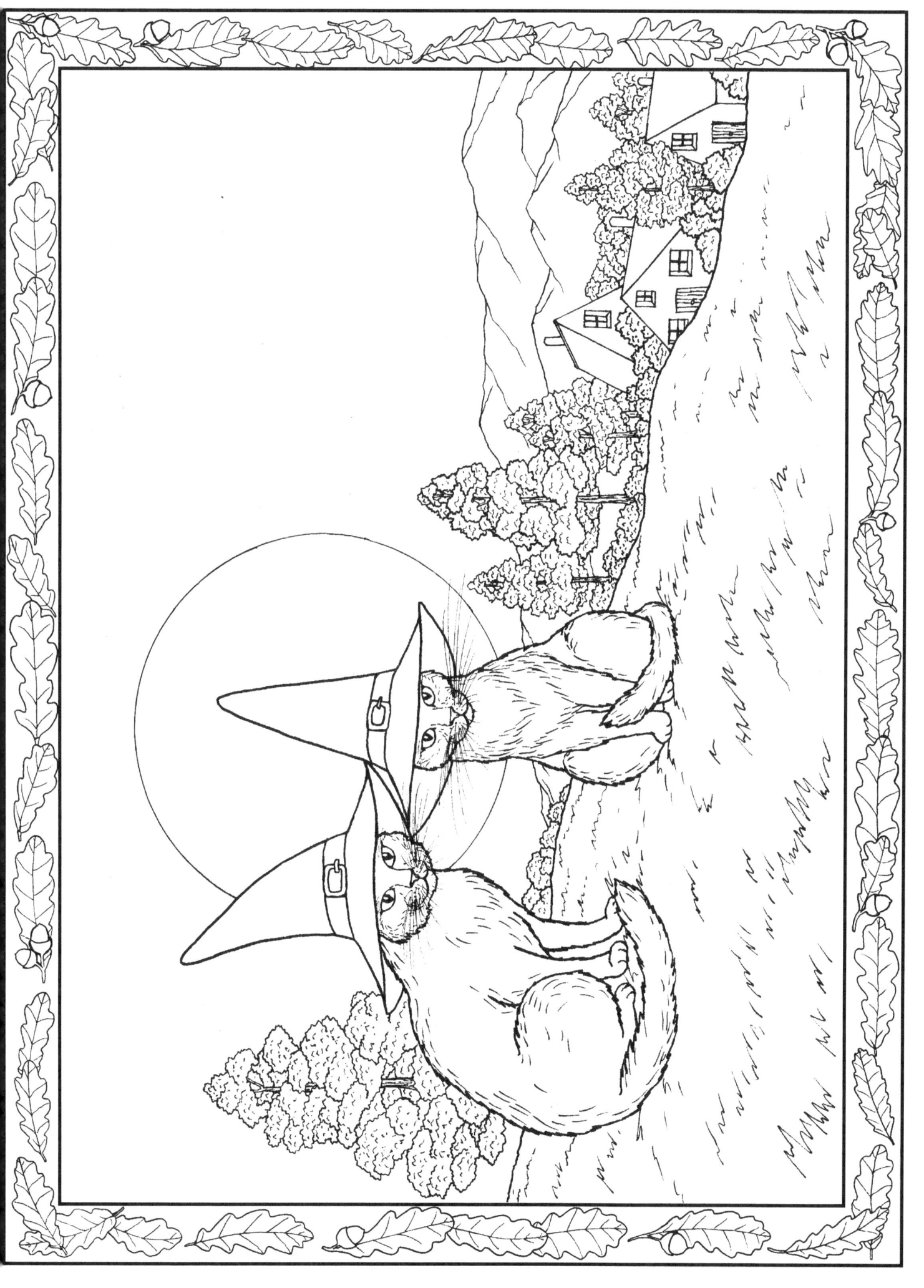

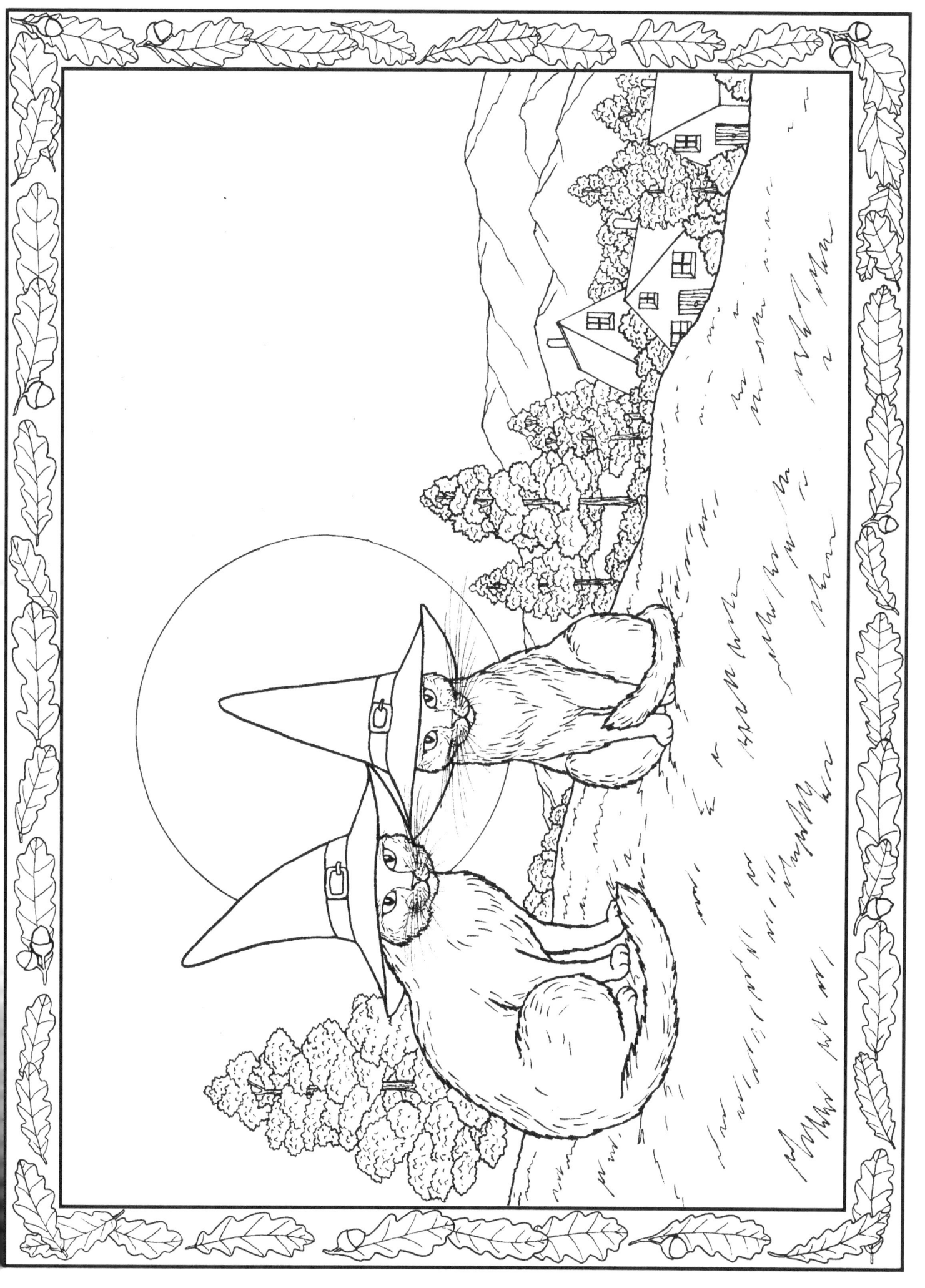

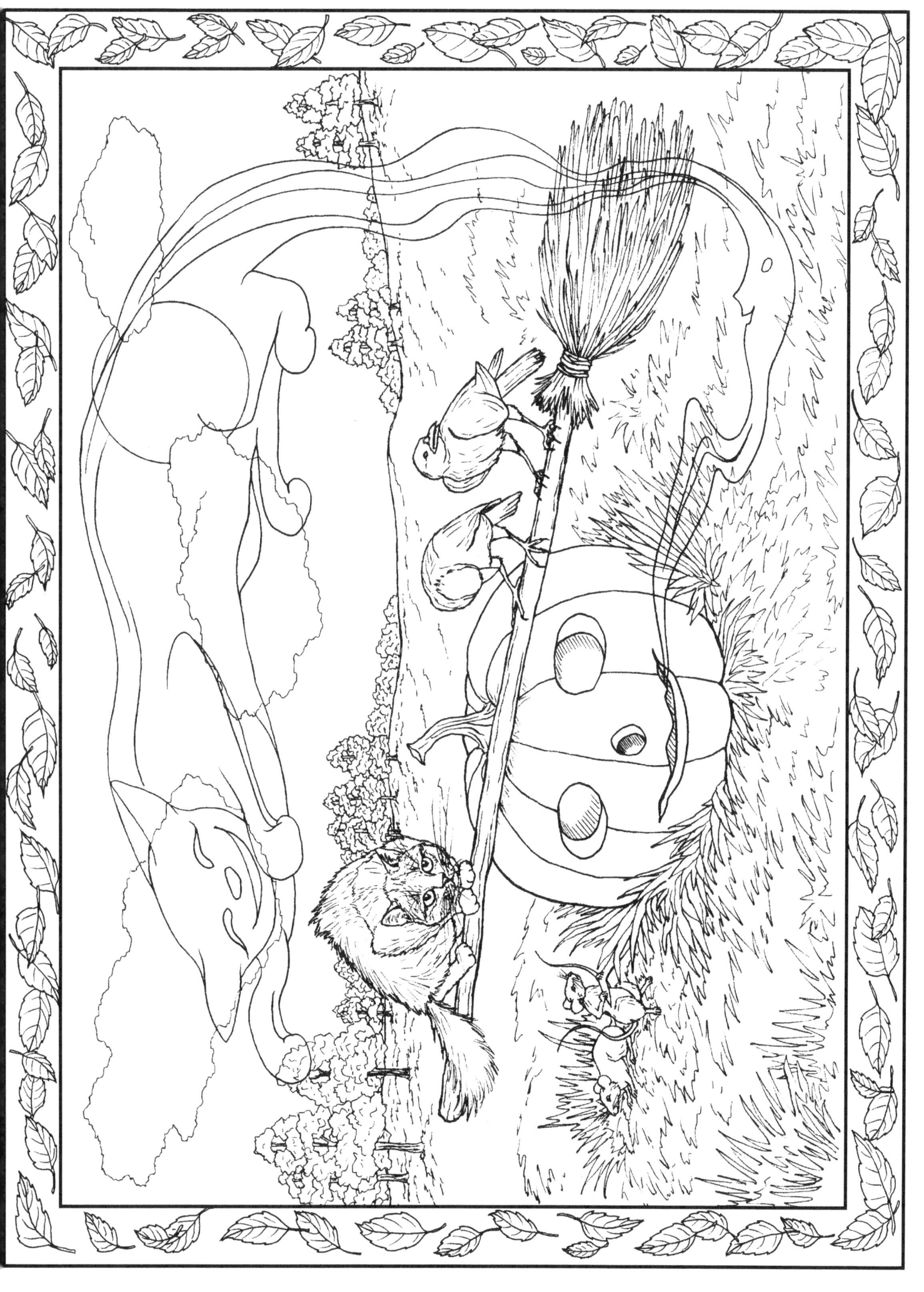

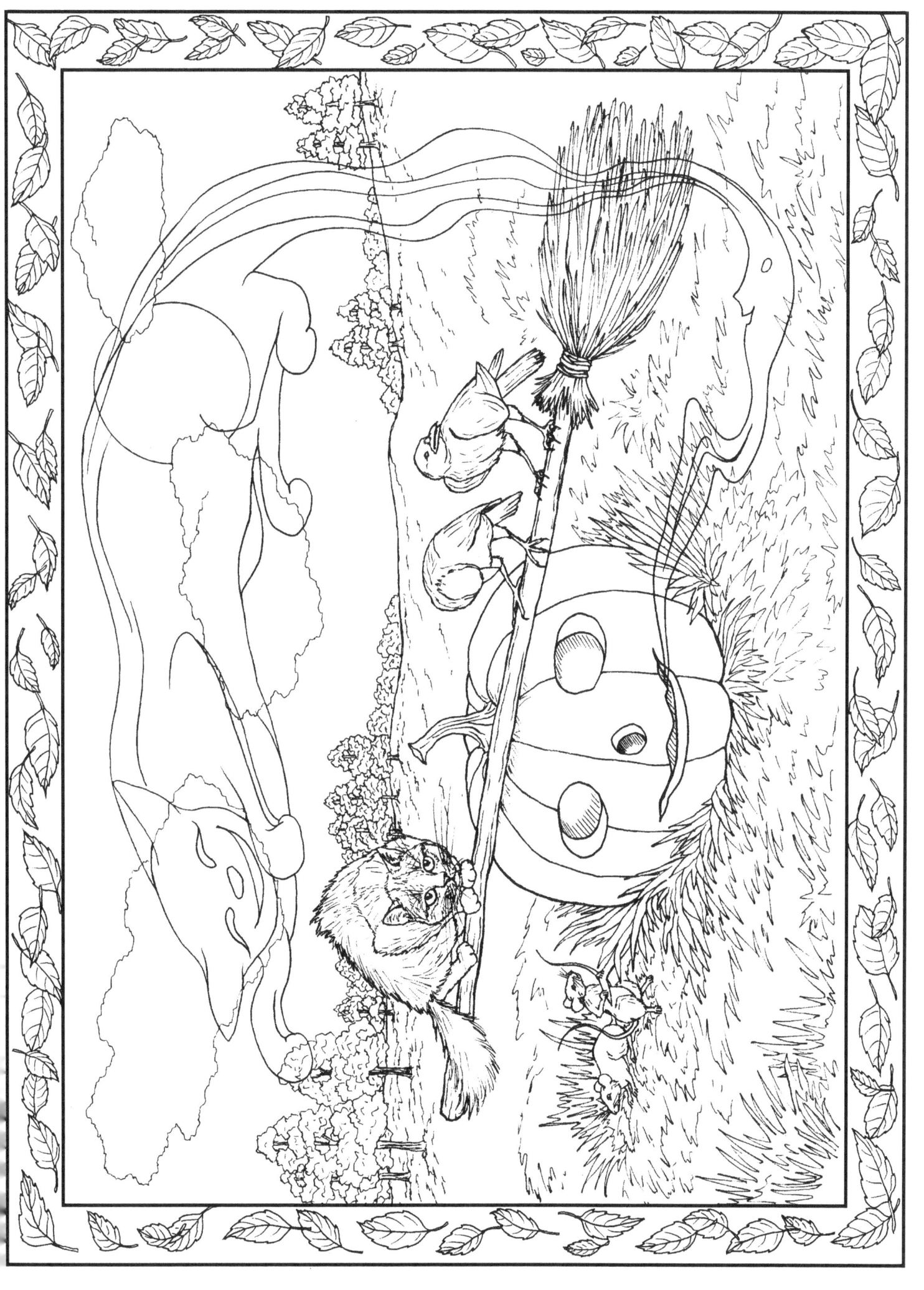

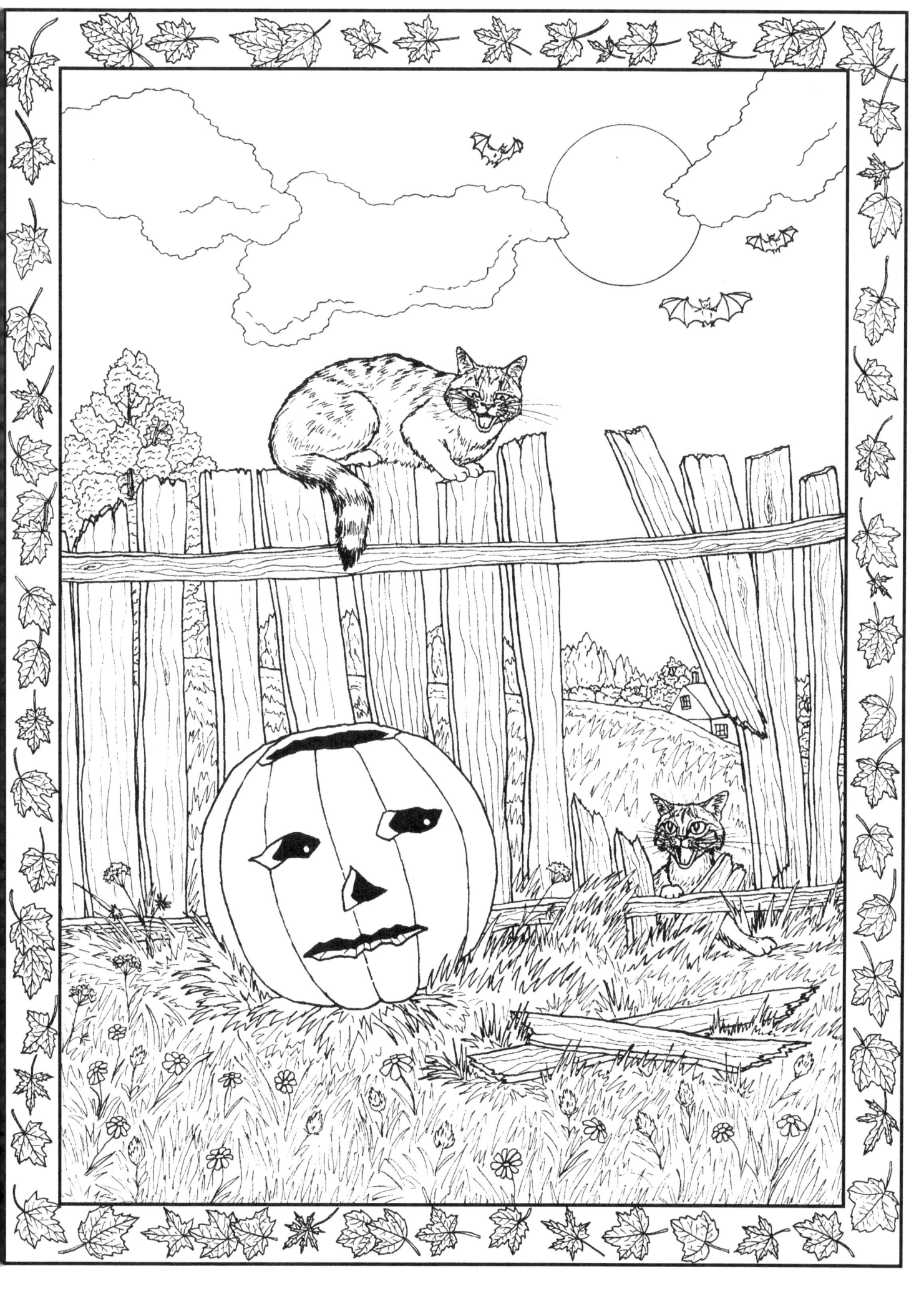

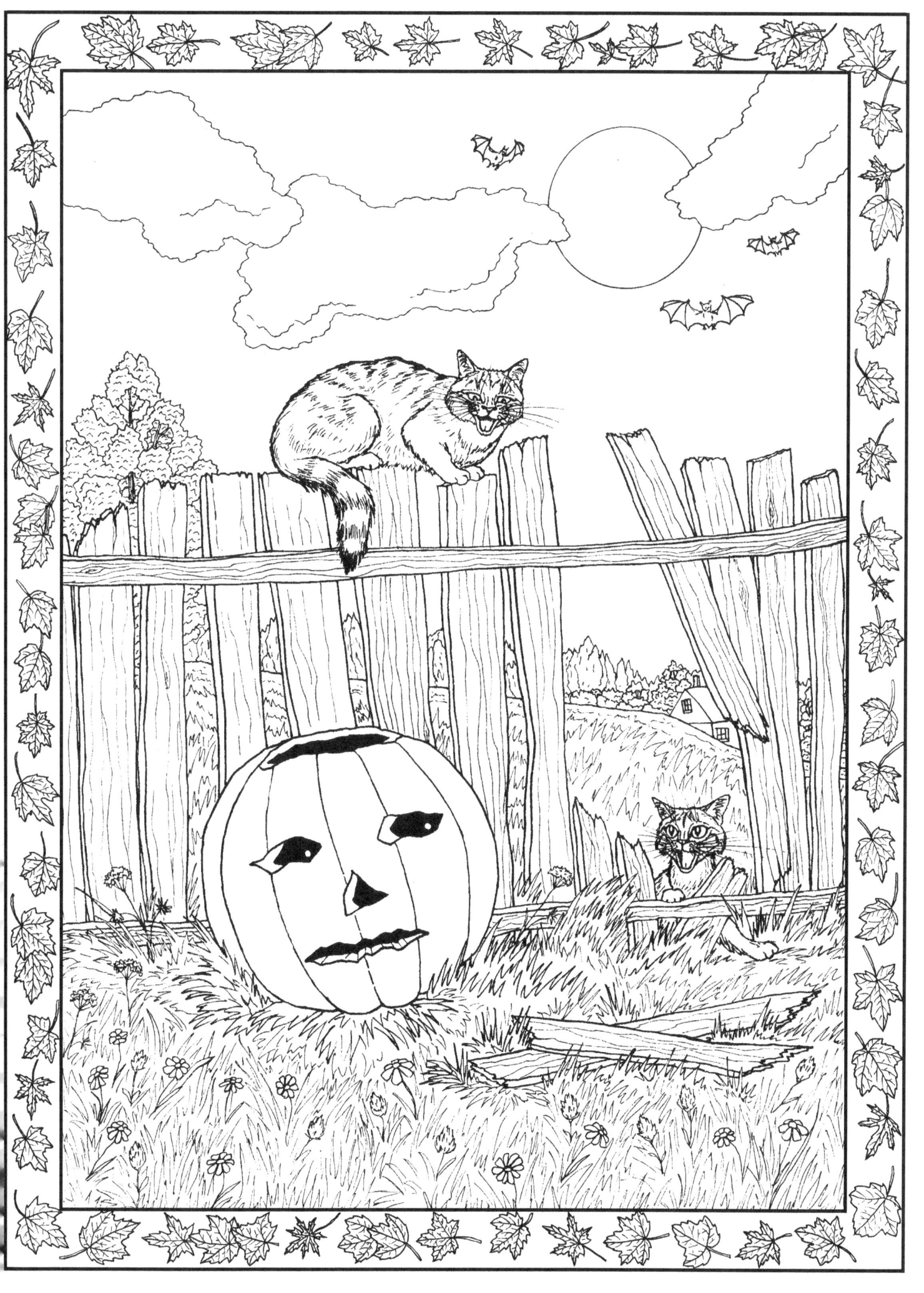

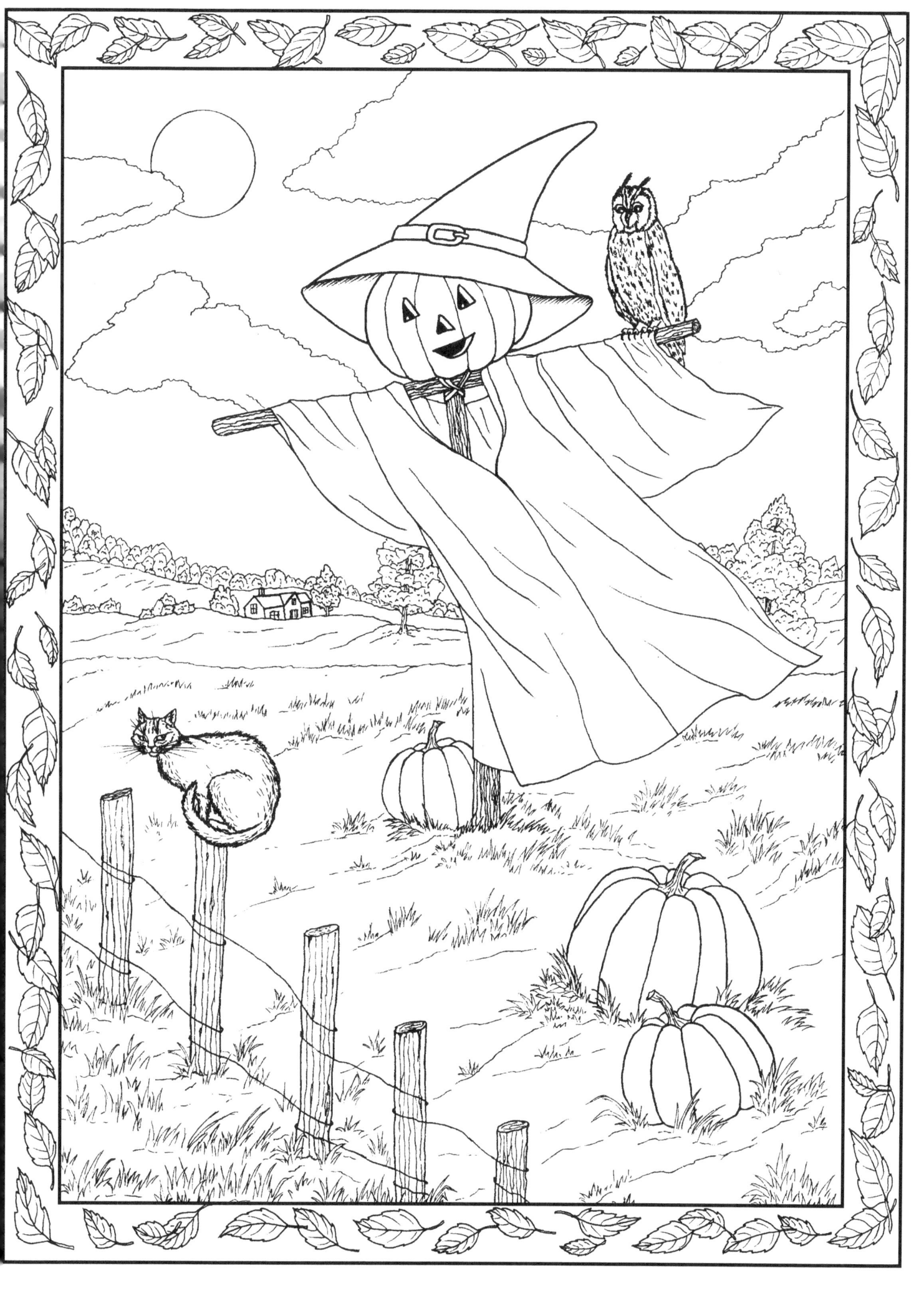

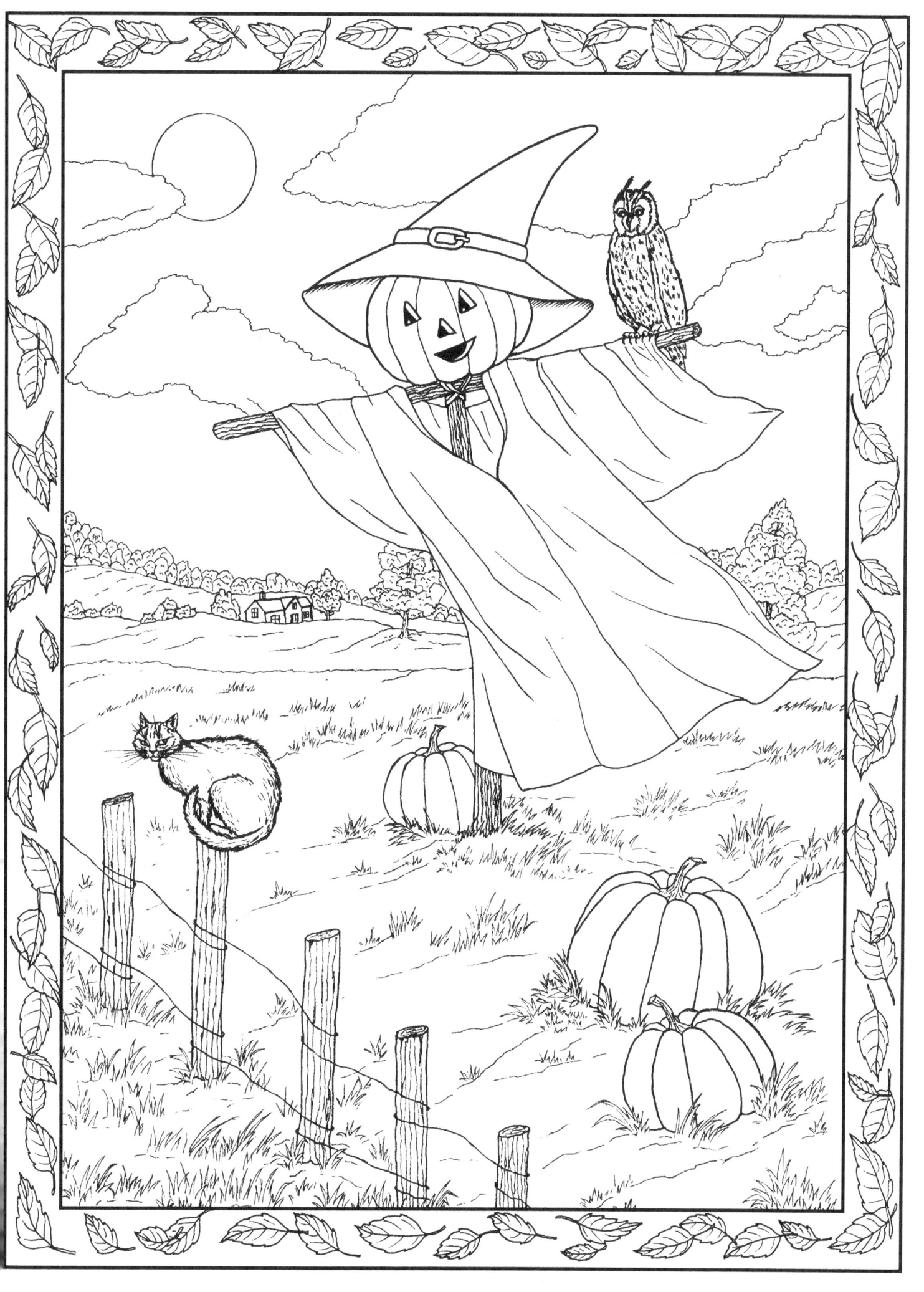

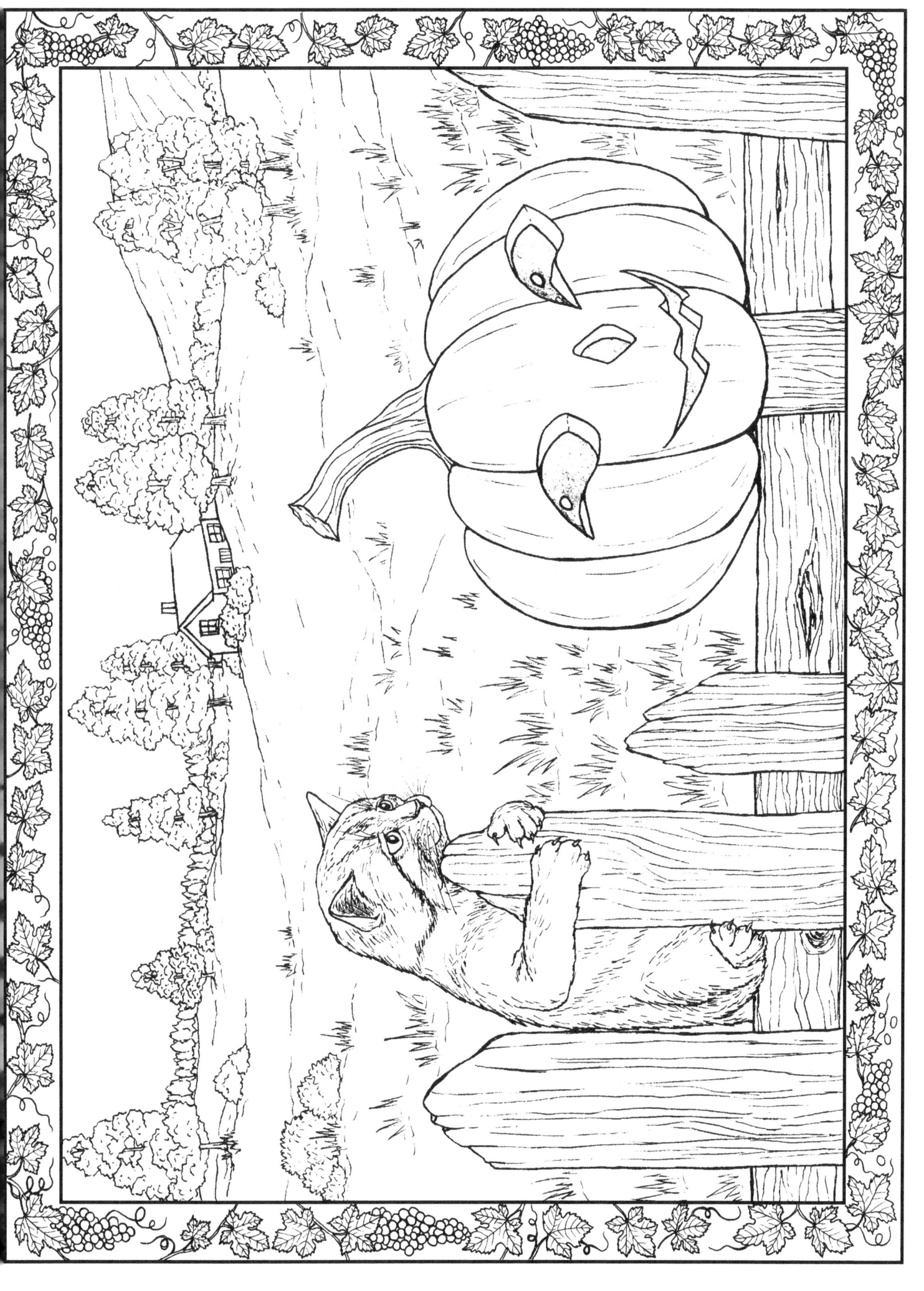

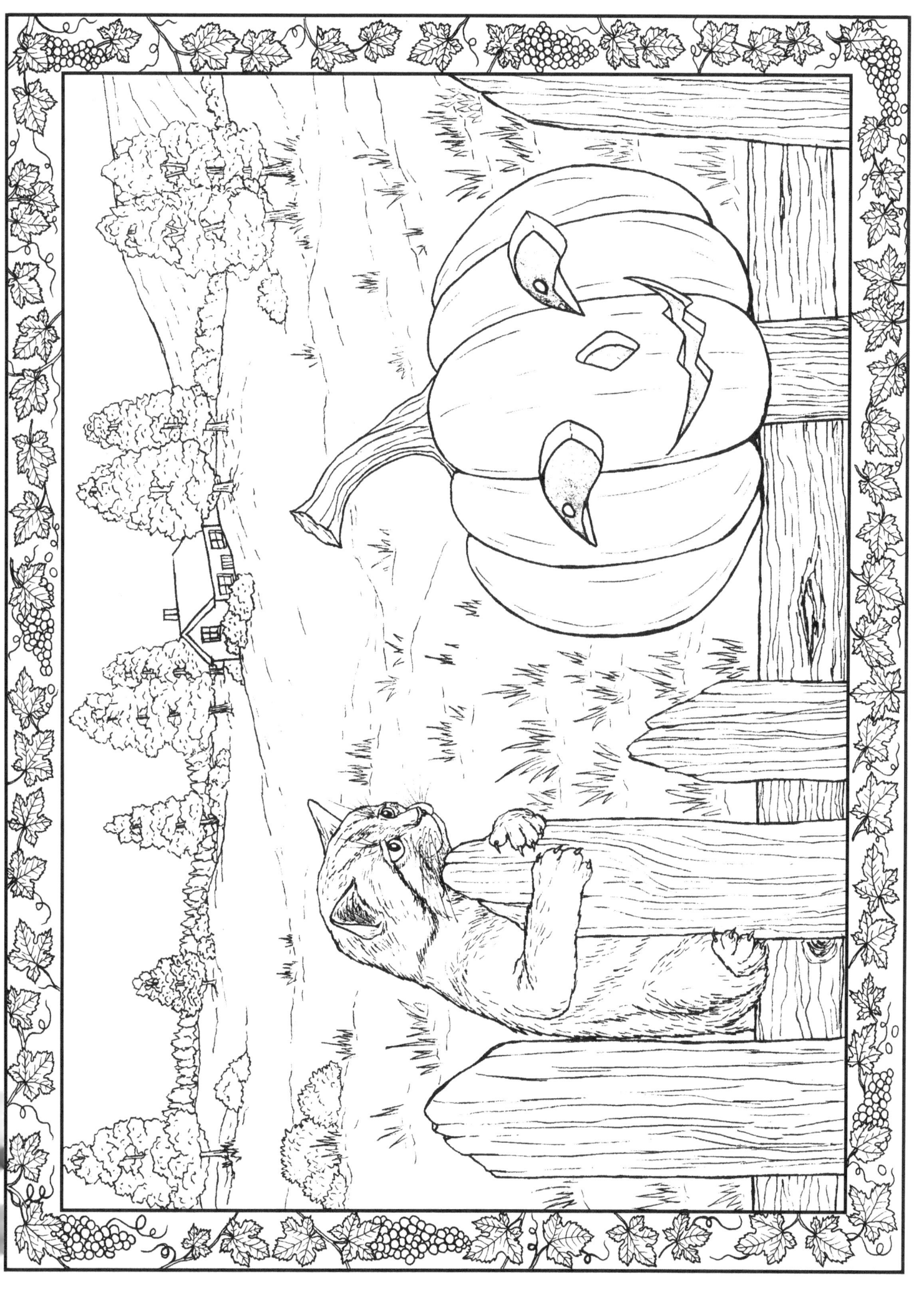

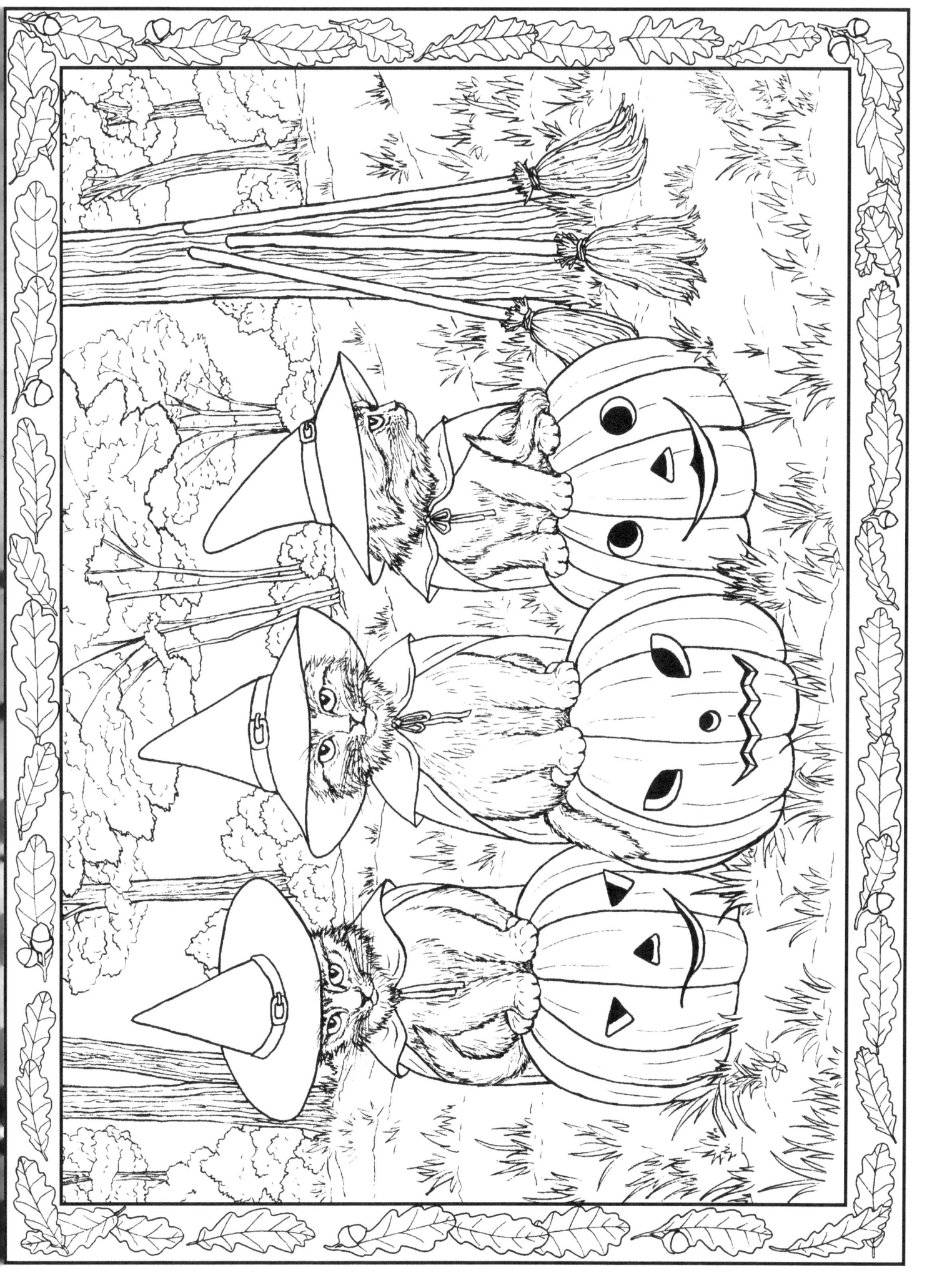

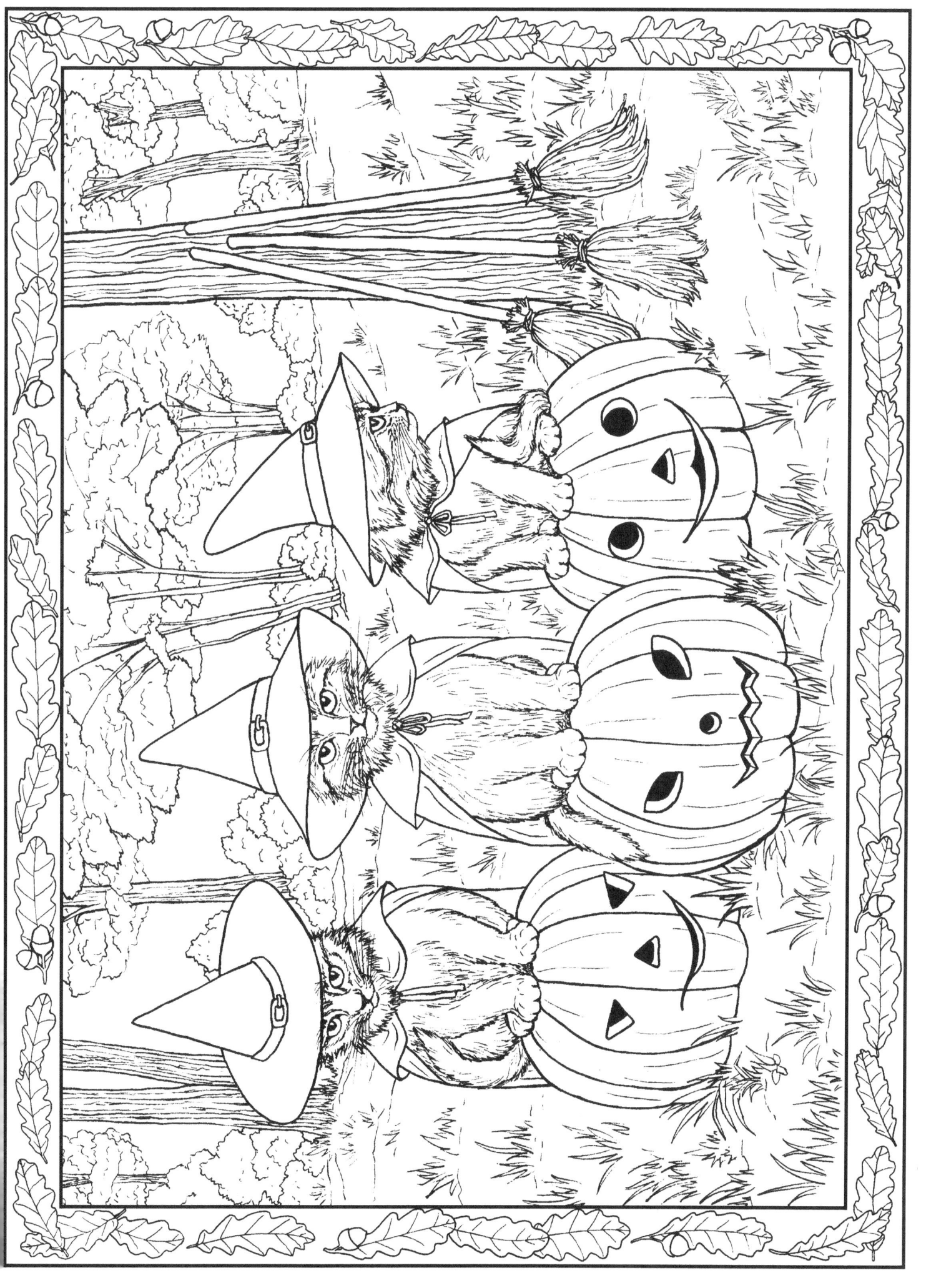